Contributions to Political Science

The book series offers an outlet for cutting-edge research in all areas of political science. Contributions to Political Science (CPS) welcomes theoretically sound and empirically robust monographs, edited volumes and handbooks from a variety of disciplines and approaches on topics such as political theory, comparative politics, democracy, European politics, electoral systems and voting behaviour, public policy and administration, political economy, and related fields.

All titles in this series are peer-reviewed. This book series is indexed in Scopus.

Wolfgang Gieler • Meik Nowak
Editors

Understanding German Development Cooperation

Motivations, Strategies and Perspectives

Springer

Editors
Wolfgang Gieler
Sozialwissenschaften
Fachhochschule Dortmund
Dortmund, Nordrhein-Westfalen, Germany

Meik Nowak
Geistes- und Sozialwissenschaften
Helmut-Schmidt-Universität
Hamburg, Hamburg, Germany

ISSN 2198-7289 ISSN 2198-7297 (electronic)
Contributions to Political Science
ISBN 978-3-658-45595-8 ISBN 978-3-658-45596-5 (eBook)
https://doi.org/10.1007/978-3-658-45596-5

This book is a translation of the original German edition "Staatliche Entwicklungszusammenarbeit in Deutschland" by Wolfgang Gieler, published by Springer Fachmedien Wiesbaden GmbH in 2021. The translation was done with the help of an artificial intelligence machine translation tool. A subsequent human revision was done primarily in terms of content, so that the book will read stylistically differently from a conventional translation. Springer Nature works continuously to further the development of tools for the production of books and on the related technologies to support the authors.

Translation from the German language edition: "Staatliche Entwicklungszusammenarbeit in Deutschland" by Wolfgang Gieler and Meik Nowak, © Der/die Herausgeber bzw. der/die Autor(en), exklusiv lizenziert an Springer Fachmedien Wiesbaden GmbH, ein Teil von Springer Nature 2021. Published by Springer Fachmedien Wiesbaden. All Rights Reserved.

© The Editor(s) (if applicable) and The Author(s), under exclusive license to Springer Fachmedien Wiesbaden GmbH, part of Springer Nature 2024

This work is subject to copyright. All rights are solely and exclusively licensed by the Publisher, whether the whole or part of the material is concerned, specifically the rights of translation, reprinting, reuse of illustrations, recitation, broadcasting, reproduction on microfilms or in any other physical way, and transmission or information storage and retrieval, electronic adaptation, computer software, or by similar or dissimilar methodology now known or hereafter developed.

The use of general descriptive names, registered names, trademarks, service marks, etc. in this publication does not imply, even in the absence of a specific statement, that such names are exempt from the relevant protective laws and regulations and therefore free for general use.

The publisher, the authors and the editors are safe to assume that the advice and information in this book are believed to be true and accurate at the date of publication. Neither the publisher nor the authors or the editors give a warranty, expressed or implied, with respect to the material contained herein or for any errors or omissions that may have been made. The publisher remains neutral with regard to jurisdictional claims in published maps and institutional affiliations.

Editorial Contact: Jan Treibel

This Springer imprint is published by the registered company Springer Fachmedien Wiesbaden GmbH, part of Springer Nature.
The registered company address is: Abraham-Lincoln-Str. 46, 65189 Wiesbaden, Germany

If disposing of this product, please recycle the paper.

Introduction

The analysis of the motives, conditions of action, strategic approaches and perspectives of German state development cooperation is essential to fully understand the dynamics and objectives of this policy arena. This analysis allows a contemporary historical investigation of the motives that led Germany to engage in development cooperation, as well as the diverse framework conditions and influencing factors that shape this policy. In doing so, not only past and current motives and patterns of action are highlighted but also future perspectives and challenges are pointed out.

Through this examination, profound insights can be gained, which serve as a basis for the further development and optimization of activities related to this policy arena. Potential obstacles and opportunities are identified to develop more effective and sustainable approaches. These insights are important not only for political decision-makers but also for practitioners and researchers in the field of development cooperation. They provide valuable insights into the current practice and provide suggestions for future strategies and measures.

Motives

German state development cooperation is a significant instrument of German foreign policy and international cooperation. The motives, conditions of action and perspectives are examined to provide a basis for understanding German development cooperation in a global context.

The motives of German state development cooperation are broadly based and reflect Germany's strategic goals and responsibilities in the international context.

- Humanitarian Responsibility:

A central driving force for German development cooperation is the moral obligation to improve living conditions and equality of opportunity in countries of the Global South. This responsibility arises from international agreements such as the human rights conventions and the awareness of the pressing global inequalities and humanitarian challenges (Crawford 2019).

- Security and Stability:

The promotion of stability in fragile regions is a significant security interest of Germany. A stable world reduces potential sources of instability, such as political conflicts and social unrest, which could negatively impact the global security situation (Brzoska 2018).

- Economic Interests:

German development cooperation also aims to open new markets and strengthen existing trade relationships. Through investments in infrastructure, education and healthcare, long-term growth is promoted, which in turn supports Germany's economic interests (Dreher et al. 2018).

- Environmental Protection and Sustainability:

Another important motive is environmental protection and the promotion of sustainability. Germany is increasingly committed to the protection of natural resources and the promotion of renewable energies in countries of the Global South, to combat climate change and promote sustainable development (GIZ 2020).

These motives are rooted in a complex interplay of humanitarian, security-related, economic and ecological factors and reflect Germany's commitment to global responsibility and sustainable development. They influence the design of German state development cooperation and show the diverse facets of this policy in the international context (Gieler & Nowak 2021).

Conditions of Action

The conditions of action of German state development cooperation are influenced by a multitude of factors, ranging from political decisions to international obligations. The following will examine these factors in more detail:

- Political framework conditions:

The priorities and objectives of German development cooperation are largely determined by international agreements and national laws. In particular, the United Nations' Agenda 2030, with its 17 Sustainable Development Goals (SDGs), forms a central reference framework for Germany's development cooperation (BMZ 2021). German development cooperation is focused on implementing the SDGs and thus contributing to the global sustainability agenda.

- Budgetary resources:

The available financial resources play a crucial role in determining the scope and implementation of development projects. The allocation of budgetary resources is priorities of partner countries are better taken into account and long-term solutions are developed.

- Innovation and knowledge exchange:

Development cooperation promotes the exchange of best practices, innovations and research results (GIZ 2020). Through the transfer of knowledge and technologies, German development activities intend to improve the effectiveness of development projects and develop new approaches. This also includes the promotion of research and innovation in areas such as healthcare, agriculture and renewable energies.

- Transformation and change:

German development cooperation aims for comprehensive societal change in partner countries (BMZ 2021). This includes promoting democratic processes, social justice and economic reforms to address structural problems and promote equal opportunities. Development cooperation is committed to sustainable socio-economic development that aims for long-term changes and contributes to improving people's living conditions.

These perspectives underline the long-term orientation and strategic goals of German state development cooperation. They demonstrate Germany's endeavors to bring about transformative changes together with partner countries and to make a positive contribution to global development.

German state development cooperation is a central instrument for promoting global development goals and reflects the complex challenges and Germany's ambitions in international cooperation. A comprehensive analysis of the motives, conditions of action, strategies and perspectives of German development cooperation allows for a deeper understanding of the significance of this area.

About the Structure of the Book

This book presents a fundamental analysis of German state development cooperation, ranging from its origins to current perspectives. It provides an in-depth insight into the historical development and evolutionary phases of this cooperation, as well as a critical examination of current trends and future directions.

The book is divided into eight structured chapters that comprehensively present the development of German state development cooperation. These chapters can be briefly outlined as follows:

1. Phases of German state development cooperation: An analysis

This chapter provides a detailed overview of the stages of German state development cooperation since its beginnings after the Second World War. It illuminates the various phases and milestones of this development, starting with the focus on reconstruction in the post-war period. Germany's state development cooperation has evolved over the decades from primary reconstruction aid to a broader sustainable development agenda that is adapted to global challenges and political changes. The presentation includes the political, economic and societal influences that have shaped these stages, as well as the changes in the structures and instruments of German development cooperation up to the present day.

2. Beginnings of (West) German development policy between continuity and priorities

Here, the early developments and priorities in (West) German development policy are analyzed and their development from the early years to the present is examined. It looks at the continuity and changes in the priorities of this policy over time. Starting with the post-war years and the focus on reconstruction after the Second World War, the first steps in German development cooperation are highlighted. It examines how the priorities have evolved over the decades, from supporting European neighbors to a global agenda for sustainable development. Particular attention is paid to the political, economic and societal influences that have shaped this development.

3. State Development Policy in the German-German Comparison: FRG and GDR

This chapter compares and examines the state development policy between the Federal Republic of Germany (FRG) and the German Democratic Republic (GDR) in the German-German context. It highlights the differences and similarities in the approaches and focuses of development cooperation in the two German states during the Cold War. In doing so, the political, ideological and economic conditions are analyzed, which have shaped the development policy in the FRG and the GDR. Special attention is paid to bilateral relations with developing countries, the forms of support and the goals of each development policy.

4. Development policy in reunified Germany between 1990 and 2021

The development of German state development policy from reunification in 1990 to the year 2021 is analyzed. It considers the transformation of development policy in a reunified Germany and examines the continuity as well as the new focuses and challenges that development cooperation faced during this period. The analysis highlights the political, economic and global influences that have shaped German development policy after reunification, including the increased integration of the former GDR into development cooperation and the orientation towards a comprehensive sustainable development agenda. Special attention is paid to Germany's role as a global actor in development cooperation, including its commitments to international agreements and goals such as the United Nations' 2030 Agenda for Sustainable Development.

5. German state development cooperation in and with fragile states

This chapter is dedicated to German state development cooperation with and in fragile states and examines the particular challenges and strategies that arise in this context. The characteristics of fragile states are discussed, including conflicts, political instability, weak institutions and high vulnerability to crises. The focus is on the approaches and measures of German development cooperation, which aim to strengthen the resilience and development capacity of fragile states and to promote long-term stability and peace. Particular attention is paid to cooperation with local actors, the promotion of governance and rule of law, and support in the areas of security, reconstruction and social services. Through this analysis, the opportunities and challenges of German state development cooperation in fragile contexts are highlighted, with a focus on sustainable solutions that aim to improve living conditions in these countries.

6. German development cooperation in the context of the Ukraine conflict

This chapter is an examination of German development cooperation in the specific context of the Ukraine conflict, including the challenges and implications. It analyzes the developments and measures that Germany has taken with regard to Ukraine and the surrounding region, especially against the backdrop of political tensions and the conflict with Russia. Special attention is paid to the specific needs and challenges of Ukraine in the development sector as well as the responses and strategies of German development cooperation. In this context, Germany's role in supporting reforms, promoting stability and addressing humanitarian challenges in the context of the Ukraine conflict is also considered.

7. The Bundeswehr as a development policy actor: A new perspective on security and development

This chapter provides a critical analysis of the role of the Bundeswehr as a unique actor in development cooperation and examines its impact on security and development. It considers the specific perspective of the Bundeswehr as a military organization in the context of development issues and analyses how this affects existing development strategies and practices. In doing so, it highlights the controversies and challenges associated with the Bundeswehr's participation in development policy measures. A focus is on the issues of security and the interaction between military and civilian actors within the framework of development cooperation.

8. Visions and strategies: The future of German governmental development cooperation

Finally, upcoming trends and challenges in German governmental development cooperation as well as possible developments are examined. It analyses the emerging perspectives for German development cooperation and considers how these could unfold against the backdrop of global changes and challenges. Central themes such as sustainability, climate change, digitalization and dealing with new and existing crises are examined in more detail. The discussion also takes into account the influence of international developments and commitments, including the implementation of the 2030 Agenda for Sustainable Development.

These chapters together provide a comprehensive insight into German governmental development cooperation by illuminating historical developments, current practices and future challenges. Through this comprehensive and well-founded presentation, the book offers an important resource for students, researchers and practitioners in the field of development cooperation. It contributes to gaining a deeper understanding of the development processes and challenges in Germany and internationally and provides impulses for future research and policy-making in this specific field.

Sozialwissenschaften Wolfgang Gieler
Fachhochschule Dortmund
Dortmund, Nordrhein-Westfalen, Germany

Geistes- und Sozialwissenschaften Meik Nowak
Helmut-Schmidt-Universität
Hamburg, Hamburg, Germany

References

Betz, J. (2021). Entwicklungspolitik: Eine Einführung in Zielsetzungen und Ergebnisse. Wiesbaden.
Bundesministerium für wirtschaftliche Zusammenarbeit und Entwicklung (BMZ). (2020). Jahresbericht Entwicklungspolitik.
Bundesministerium für wirtschaftliche Zusammenarbeit und Entwicklung (BMZ). (2021). Strategiepapier Entwicklungspolitik.
Bräutigam, D., & Knack, S. (2020). Foreign Aid, Institutions, and Governance in Sub-Saharan Africa. Journal of International Development, 32 (5), 589–613.
Brzoska, M. (2018). Germany's strategic culture and international security: Between pacifism and interventionism. Palgrave Macmillan, Cham.
Crawford, G. (2019). The case for the international development aid programme. The Lancet Global Health, 7 (11), 1410–1412.
Dreher, A., Eichenauer, V. Z., & Gehring, K. (2018). Geopolitics, aid, and growth: The impact of UN Security Council membership. World Development, 112, 59–77.
Deutsche Gesellschaft für Internationale Zusammenarbeit (GIZ). (2020). Development Cooperation Strategy Report.
Ewers, M. (2017). The Logic of Practical Norms: A Case Study of Development Cooperation in International Biodiversity Law. London.
Gieler, W., & Nowak, M. (2021). Staatliche Entwicklungszusammenarbeit in Deutschland: Eine Bestandsaufnahme des BMZ 1961–2021. Wiesbaden.

Contents

1 **Phases of German State Development Cooperation: An Analysis** 1
Wolfgang Gieler and Meik Nowak

2 **Beginnings of (West) German Development Policy Between Continuity and Priorities** 13
Wolfgang Gieler

3 **State Development Policy in German-German Comparison: FRG and GDR** 29
Wolfgang Gieler

4 **Development Policy in Reunified Germany Between 1990 and 2021** 47
Meik Nowak

5 **German State Development Cooperation in and with Fragile States** 69
Meik Nowak

6 **German Development Cooperation in the Context of the Ukraine Conflict** 81
Wolfgang Gieler and Meik Nowak

7 **The Bundeswehr as Actor in the Field of Developmental Policy: A New Perspective on Security and Development** 91
Meik Nowak

8 **Visions and Strategies: The Future of German Government Development Cooperation** 107
Meik Nowak

Appendix 127

Chapter 1
Phases of German State Development Cooperation: An Analysis

Wolfgang Gieler and Meik Nowak

Abstract This paper has examined the milestones of German state development cooperation since the 1960s and its role in the context of German foreign policy. Over time, development cooperation has evolved from humanitarian aid and infrastructure development in countries of the Global South to a more strategic orientation with long-term development policy goals. The reunification of Germany in the 1990s brought about comprehensive restructuring, including the integration of the new federal states and a stronger focus on regional cooperation. Particular attention is paid to the strategic goals, institutional changes, and priorities of German development cooperation. It now also includes the promotion of self-responsibility, good governance, and economic development. Present trends such as climate change, conflicts, and migration pose new challenges.

In the discussion about international relations and global solidarity, the terms development aid, development policy, and development cooperation play a central role. But what exactly do they mean? These terms are fundamental concepts in the context of international cooperation. Their differences and meanings are of great importance for the design of strategies to promote global development and combat economic poverty and inequality.

W. Gieler (✉)
Sozialwissenschaften, Fachhochschule Dortmund, Dortmund, Nordrhein-Westfalen, Germany
e-mail: wolfgang.gieler@fh-dortmund.de

M. Nowak
Geistes- und Sozialwissenschaften, Helmut-Schmidt-Universität, Hamburg, Hamburg, Germany
e-mail: nowakme@hsu-hh.de

© The Author(s), under exclusive license to Springer Fachmedien Wiesbaden GmbH, part of Springer Nature 2024
W. Gieler, M. Nowak (eds.), *Understanding German Development Cooperation*, Contributions to Political Science, https://doi.org/10.1007/978-3-658-45596-5_1

Development Policy: Fundamentals, Terms, and Historical Evolution

Development aid refers to the targeted provision of resources such as financial support, technical expertise, and training by wealthier countries or organisations for the benefit of economically poorer countries or communities. Its aim is to improve living conditions and promote basic needs such as healthcare, education, and infrastructure.

Development policy is a long-term strategic orientation at national and international level, aimed at addressing the structural causes of economic poverty and inequality. It includes political measures, programmes, and reforms to promote sustainable development in economically poorer countries. This includes investments in education, health, infrastructure, as well as the promotion of good governance and economic opportunities.

Development cooperation refers to the cooperative partnership between various actors such as governments, international organisations, non-governmental organisations (NGOs), and the private sector, to promote development in economically poorer countries. The focus is on capacity building and strengthening self-help to achieve sustainable development. Development cooperation includes financial support, technical assistance, knowledge exchange, and the establishment of institutional structures (Gieler and Schwarz 2020, 14–19).

The terms development aid, development policy, and development cooperation are closely related concepts that together aim for positive development in economically poorer countries. While development aid focuses on concrete assistance, development policy emphasises structural changes and reforms. Development cooperation emphasises partnership cooperation and capacity building for sustainable development. A comprehensive understanding of these concepts can develop effective strategies for promoting global development and achieving development policy goals.

Historians usually place the beginning of (international) development policy in the 1920s, considering this in the context of late colonialism and the crisis of the former colonial empires of Britain and France. At this time, the League of Nations was already dealing with transferring the former Ottoman and German colonies to mandate powers and providing them with development mandates (Giessmann 2005, 123–145).

Contrary to other disciplines, political science typically identifies the emergence of (international) development policy as beginning in the period following the Second World War. A key document in this context is the inaugural address of 20 January 1949 by then US President Harry S. Truman, in which he announced the founding of the North Atlantic Treaty Organization (NATO).

> In addition, we will provide military advice and equipment to free nations which will cooperate with us in the maintenance of peace and security. Fourth, we must embark on a bold new program for making the benefits of our scientific advances and industrial progress available for the improvement and growth of underdeveloped areas. More than half the

people of the world are living in conditions approaching misery. Their food is inadequate. They are victims of disease. Their economic life is primitive and stagnant. Their poverty is a handicap and a threat both to them and to more prosperous areas. For the first time in history, humanity possesses the knowledge and skill to relieve the suffering of these people. (Truman 1949)

Over the past decades, the focus of development cooperation has changed, but the development policy models have followed global trends, which were mainly determined by the balance of power of the internationally leading political and economic countries. Particular attention still deserves the existing unequal relationship between the countries of the Global North and the Global South. This monocentrism is evident in the definition of development- or aid-needy countries and the underlying criteria. The framework conditions of today's relationships between the Global North and the Global South are essentially based on this foundation (Gieler 2023, 13ff).

The terms "Global North" and "Global South" are not understood solely geographically but serve as a value-neutral description of different positions in a globalised world. A country of the Global South is considered socially, politically, and economically disadvantaged, while a country of the Global North occupies a privileged position. These terms are used to avoid a hierarchy between "economically developed countries" and "developing countries".

It is pleasing to note that the terms "Global North" and "Global South" are now established among non-governmental organisations in the field of German development cooperation, especially in the development policy education and some humanities disciplines. In contrast, these terms are still firmly anchored in the language use of state institutions and organisations in Germany such as the Society for International Cooperation (GIZ) or the Federal Ministry for Economic Cooperation and Development (BMZ) (Gieler 2023, 26f).

The history of development policy—and thus also of German development policy—is and remains characterised by the intertwining of various policy areas, including foreign, foreign economic, education, health, migration, environmental, and security policy. The origins of German development cooperation can be traced back historically to the 1950s although systematic coordination only began with the founding of the Federal Ministry for Economic Cooperation in 1961. At this time, the Federal Ministry for Economic Affairs (BMWi) was the first to recognise the newly emerged task of development cooperation and also implemented the first state development projects.

In the 1950s, Germany was heavily destroyed after the Second World War and faced major economic challenges. It became clear that in addition to national reconstruction work there was also an international responsibility, especially towards the former colonies and other developing countries. The BMWi took a pioneering role and began with the first state initiatives to promote development cooperation.

The actual systematic coordination and institutional anchoring of these efforts then took place with the founding of the independent Federal Ministry for Economic Cooperation in 1961. This marked an important step in German development policy and laid the foundation for a long-term and strategic orientation of the development policy activities of the Federal Republic of Germany.

Since then, German state development cooperation has changed and now encompasses a wide range of measures and programmes to promote sustainable development in partner countries worldwide. The history and development of German state development cooperation also reflects international developments and the change in development policy priorities over time.

In 1953, the Federal Ministry for Economic Affairs (BMWi) received half a million Deutschmarks under the European Recovery Program (ERP) initiated by US Secretary of State General George Catlett Marshall. These funds were intended for the exchange of experiences with economically less developed areas. However, a condition for the allocation of these funds was the promotion of the West German economy. As a result, the concept of technical assistance from 1954 took on more the function of long-term trade and export promotion for West Germany.

The consolidation of post-war economies and the growing East-West confrontation led to the Western European states increasingly orienting their national policies on the model of the USA. The so-called "Marshall Plan" ERP programme was essentially based on the economic interests of the USA and served as an instrument for implementing geopolitical strategies. This illustrates the extent to which the newly emerging development policy was tied to the (foreign) economic interests of the donor countries.

Within the framework of the ERP programme, development cooperation was strongly linked to the goals of promoting the West German economy and the strategic interests of the USA. Technical assistance and the exchange of experiences were ultimately intended to promote economic stability in West Germany and strengthen the position of the USA in the geopolitical landscape of the Cold War.

This development illustrates the connection between development policy, economic promotion, and geopolitical strategy in the post-war period. It shows how the emerging development cooperation in Germany and other Western European states was closely linked to global power relations and the interests of the leading industrial nations.

In the wake of the economic challenges of numerous politically independent states, the Bundestag approved a sum of 50 million marks for technical assistance to the Foreign Office (AA) 2 years later. This decision was guided by humanitarian considerations and was based on the concept of the Point Four Program of US President Harry S. Truman. A central development policy aspect of this programme was the idea that the "developed" industrial countries should help the "underdeveloped" countries to help themselves.

However, both the Federal Ministry for Economic Affairs (BMWi) and the Foreign Office (AA) lacked a clear development policy concept. This lack of concept was exacerbated by a conflict over the distribution of available financial resources and the respective priorities of cooperation between the BMWi and the AA. While the BMWi primarily aimed at trade and export policy goals that served its own foreign trade, the AA saw development policy measures primarily as an instrument for enforcing the Hallstein Doctrine.

The Hallstein Doctrine proclaimed a legally justified claim to sole representation of the Federal Republic of Germany for all of Germany and established itself in the course of the 1950s as a fundamental foreign policy principle of the Federal Republic. In view of the East-West conflict, the Federal Republic regarded the establishment of diplomatic relations by a state with the GDR as an "unfriendly act" and in turn ended diplomatic relations with the respective country.

The historical context described illustrates the complex connection between development cooperation, foreign policy interests, and the global power play during the Cold War. The USA recognised early on that combating communism required not only military and political measures but also stabilisation and development of economically weak regions. This approach was reflected in the demand for "burden sharing", where the Federal Republic of Germany should play a crucial role as a prosperous nation (Gieler and Nowak 2021, V–XVIII).

The creation of new development policy institutions in Germany underlines the country's growing commitment to development cooperation. These efforts were motivated both by strategic considerations in the East-West conflict and by the desire for global stability. The idea that economic poverty could be a breeding ground for communist ideologies significantly drove this policy.

The Federal Republic of Germany responded to pressure from the USA by intensifying its development policy efforts. This step was closely linked to foreign policy and power political interests during the Cold War. It also shows how development cooperation became a tool in the geopolitical power play to contain the influence of communism and strengthen global security. The German foreign policy goals of Western integration and the restoration of sovereignty after the Second World War had significant impacts on development policy activities during the Adenauer era. This era was characterised by a close link between development policy decisions and the strategic goals of the Federal Republic of Germany.

A significant example of this was Germany's participation in the Colombo Plan in 1953. The Colombo Plan was a British initiative to coordinate economic support for countries in South and Southeast Asia. Germany's participation in this plan was not only a development policy step but also an important step towards strengthening international cooperation and integration into the Western world. It demonstrated Germany's commitment to the common goals of the Western powers in development aid and strengthened the Federal Republic's position as a reliable partner in the context of Western integration.

Another significant example was the French-German Treaty of 16 July 1954. The treaty provided for the provision of 200 million marks of German support for an overseas development fund, which primarily benefited the French colonies. This treaty was part of broader efforts to strengthen French-German relations and solidify Western solidarity on the Germany question, particularly during the Cold War and post-war period. Germany's support for the Overseas Development Fund was both a political signal of solidarity with France and a step towards strengthening Germany's presence in international development cooperation.

Overall, these examples reflect the complex interplay between development policy objectives and foreign policy interests during the Adenauer era. The Federal

Republic of Germany used its development policy activities as a means to achieve its strategic foreign policy goals, particularly Western integration and the preservation of its sovereignty. These interconnections highlight the importance of the development policy dimension for German foreign policy in a time of geopolitical change and the consolidation of the Western alliance after the Second World War (Gieler and Nowak 2021, VII–XVIII).

The periodisation of the Federal Republic of Germany's state development cooperation based on the terms of office of the ministers of the Federal Ministry for Economic Cooperation and Development (BMZ) provides insights into the historical development and changing priorities of this policy.

Early Phase (1950s to Early 1960s)

The early phase of the Federal Republic of Germany's state development cooperation in the 1950s to the early 1960s marked a crucial step in the establishment and institutionalisation of this policy as a significant instrument of German foreign policy after the Second World War. Germany was in a geopolitically unstable environment of the Cold War at this time, which reinforced the need for a clear international role and cooperation.

A crucial aspect of this phase was the close cooperation with former colonial powers such as Great Britain and France. These partnerships were of great importance as they facilitated the establishment of networks and the setting of political guidelines for development cooperation. Germany sought to establish its development policy on a solid foundation and at the same time strengthen its position in the international arena.

The ministers of this time, such as Walter Scheel (1961–1966), Werner Dollinger (1966–1966), and Hans-Jürgen Wischnewski (1966–1968), played a decisive role in shaping this phase. They worked to create institutional foundations that set the new political framework for development cooperation. This included not only the provision of financial support but also the definition of clear goals and strategies to promote the political interests of Germany at the international level.

This early period laid the foundation for the further development of West German state development cooperation. It was characterised by a process of construction and the search for international recognition and influence. The experiences and achievements of this phase had a lasting impact on the following development phases. They contributed to making German development cooperation a recognised and important instrument of foreign policy in the global context, which was of great importance both at the strategic level and in practice (Gieler and Nowak 2021, 3–41).

Growth and Diversification Phase (1960s to 1980s)

The phase of growth and diversification of West German state development cooperation in the 1960s to the 1980s was a time of significant expansion and deepening of this policy. Germany expanded its development cooperation geographically and included new partner countries in Africa, Asia, and Latin America. As a result, the network and sphere of influence of German development policy expanded considerably (Unmüssig 1999, 321–339).

A central focus in this phase was on promoting social and economic development in the partner countries. This included measures to improve education, healthcare, and infrastructure, to promote sustainable development goals and improve the living conditions of the population. Germany emphasised a holistic development cooperation that not only targeted economic aspects but also considered social and humanitarian concerns.

Ministers such as Erhard Eppler (1968–1974), Egon Bahr (1974–1976), and Marie Schlei (1976–1978) played a crucial role in the expansion and diversification of this policy. Eppler promoted a comprehensive development agenda and the integration of new partner countries. Schlei expanded the geographical and thematic orientation of cooperation, particularly through increased consideration of social and humanitarian issues (Schneckener 2007, 61–75).

Overall, this phase marked a significant growth period for German development cooperation, characterised by a broader geographical presence and a more comprehensive approach to promoting sustainable development. The efforts of this time laid the foundation for a continued extensive and diverse development cooperation of Germany, which went beyond purely economic concerns and also included social and humanitarian aspects (Gieler and Nowak 2021, 43–96).

Consolidation Phase and Focus Setting (Late 1980s to 1990s)

The consolidation phase of West German state development cooperation in the late 1980s to the 1990s was characterised by a conscious focus on strategic partnerships and long-term development goals. During this time, environmental and sustainability aspects as well as poverty reduction and global justice increasingly came into focus.

The context of this phase was characterised by a growing realisation that addressing global development issues such as economic poverty and environmental destruction required a coordinated, long-term approach. German development policy responded by expanding its focus and developing programmes that aimed not only at short-term aid but also at structural changes to promote sustainable development.

Key players such as Ministers Jürgen Warnke and Carl-Dieter Spranger played a significant role in the realignment of development cooperation. Under their leadership, the promotion of environmental protection and sustainability became an integral part of German development policy. The need to integrate environmental aspects into development projects was recognised in order to secure the livelihoods of people in partner countries in the long term.

A main goal was to establish long-term and partnership-based relationships with developing countries that went beyond purely financial or technical aid. German development cooperation aimed to strengthen capacities and structures in partner countries in order to achieve a sustainable improvement in living conditions.

The consolidation phase marked a strategic shift towards a more comprehensive consideration of environmental and sustainability aspects as well as poverty reduction and global justice. This approach helped to increase the effectiveness and relevance of German development cooperation and to promote long-term development goals that went beyond purely economic objectives. It was a time of rethinking and integrating new priorities into German development policy, which continues to shape it today (Gieler and Nowak 2021, 111–165).

Modernisation and Global Challenges (2000s to 2015)

The phase of modernisation and addressing global challenges in German development cooperation, which extended from the 2000s to around 2015, was characterised by an adaptation to changing global conditions such as globalisation, climate change, and digital transformation. This era was marked by a close linkage of development cooperation with other policy areas such as trade, security, and migration. In addition, the promotion of partnerships with non-governmental organisations (NGOs) and the private sector gained importance.

The adaptation to global conditions reflected the need to adjust development cooperation to the new global realities. The increasing influence of globalisation required enhanced cooperation between countries of the Global North and the Global South to manage the impacts on trade, environment, and social conditions. Climate change, in particular, was recognised as one of the greatest global challenges, leading to increased measures to promote climate protection and adaptation in development cooperation (Hentges 2015, 367–382).

The close linkage with other policy areas was a prominent change during this phase. Development policy measures were increasingly seen as an integral part of a broader strategy to promote peace, security, and sustainable development. This reflected the understanding that addressing global challenges requires an integrated approach that goes beyond traditional development policy measures.

The promotion of partnerships with NGOs and the private sector also gained importance. NGOs were often able to respond more flexibly to local needs and played a crucial role in implementing development projects. At the same time, cooperation with the private sector mobilised innovation and resources to achieve sustainable development goals and stimulate economic impulses in countries of the Global South.

Federal Minister Heidemarie Wieczorek-Zeul and Federal Minister Gerd Müller played a central role in the modernisation of German state development cooperation. They drove the promotion of innovative partnerships and approaches to adapt the effectiveness and relevance of German development policy to the challenges of the twenty-first century. Their work contributed to making Germany's development cooperation more effective and future-oriented by responding to changing global conditions and developing new cooperation models.

Overall, this phase was characterised by a time of adaptation and renewal in German development cooperation, aimed at effectively addressing global challenges and strengthening development cooperation through innovative partnerships and integrated policy approaches. This strategic change laid the foundation for a continued relevant and effective German state development policy in the international context (Gieler and Nowak 2021, 167–231).

Adaptive Strategies: German Development Policy from 2015 to 2024 Adaptation to Worldwide Developments and Political Priorities

The periodisation of German development policy from 2015 to 2024 illustrates the dynamic adaptations to global developments, challenges, and political priorities during this period. German development cooperation responded flexibly to present global challenges and political priorities by continuously adapting its strategies and focuses.

From 2015 to 2017, a particular focus was on the implementation of the United Nations' Sustainable Development Goals (SDGs) in the countries of the Global South. German state development cooperation intensified its efforts to combat poverty, promote education and healthcare, and build sustainable infrastructures. The implementation of the SDGs was at the centre of many projects and initiatives by the BMZ, aimed at sustainably improving living conditions in countries of the Global South. The promotion of the SDGs was a fundamental cornerstone of German development policy in this phase (Mair 2017, 189–205).

From 2018 to 2020, climate protection became increasingly important as a central aspect of German state development cooperation. In the face of the growing threat of climate change, Germany increasingly focused on measures to promote the resilience of countries in the Global South. German state development cooperation during this time focused on promoting climate-resilient infrastructures, sustainable agricultural practices, and support for adaptation to changed climatic conditions. These measures were intended to help strengthen the resilience of countries in the Global South to the impacts of climate change (Schmidt 2020 45–51).

The term of office of Federal Minister Svenja Schulze since 2021 has been characterised by a strong promotion of digital innovations and technologies in German development cooperation. The focus is on using digital solutions to increase the efficiency and effectiveness of development projects. Germany supports digital education initiatives, the expansion of digital health services, and the promotion of digital platforms to improve access to financial services in countries of the Global South. These measures are intended to facilitate access to modern technologies and promote innovative solutions to development problems in order to achieve the 17 Sustainable Development Goals of the UN Agenda 2030 (BMZ 2022).

Another goal of Minister Swenja Schultze's term of office is the promotion of equal political, economic, and social participation of all people, regardless of gender, gender identity, and sexual orientation. To this end, a comprehensive "Gender Action Plan" is being developed, aimed at addressing gender-related inequalities and discrimination in various areas.

The Gender Action Plan is intended to contain specific measures and strategies to promote equal opportunities and equality in politics, promoting economy and society. This could include the introduction of quota regulations in politics and economy, strengthening the rights of LGBTQ+ individuals, promoting education and employment opportunities for women and people with different gender identities, and raising awareness for gender-specific issues and combating prejudices.

The Gender Action Plan is based on international commitments such as the UN Sustainable Development Goals and the promotion of gender equality, as well as national laws and initiatives to promote equality. It is developed in collaboration with various stakeholders such as NGOs, scientists, civil society, and international organisations to ensure a comprehensive and effective implementation. The development and implementation of such a Gender Action Plan is crucial for the long-term promotion of equality and participation in Germany and contributes to creating a fairer and more inclusive society and economic system (BMZ 2021).

The COVID-19 pandemic had profound consequences on German state development cooperation from 2020 and reinforced the importance of health systems, crisis response measures, and digital solutions. The pandemic led to increased efforts, to strengthen the resilience of health systems in countries of the Global South and the use of digital tools.

The present Ukraine war has significant impacts on the German state development cooperation. One of the main consequences is the redistribution of resources within German development cooperation to provide humanitarian aid and support in the affected regions of Ukraine and the neighbouring countries. This has led to a possible realignment of financial priorities and resource distribution to address the acute needs of the population affected by conflicts.

In addition, the Ukraine war has influenced Germany's political priorities in the field of development cooperation. Certain countries or regions may have been brought more into focus to promote stability, security, and sustainable development, especially against the backdrop of geopolitical changes in Europe due to the conflict.

The importance of security aspects in German state development cooperation has increased, as the conflict in Ukraine has affected the overall security situation in Europe. Germany may take more measures to strengthen the resilience of communities in conflict regions and address the causes of conflicts to promote long-term stability and development.

The Ukraine war has also led to increased flight and migration, which has changed the requirements and priorities of German state development cooperation. Specifically, the assistance provided to refugees and displaced persons, along with efforts to promote their integration.

International cooperation and diplomacy are also important aspects that have been influenced by the Ukraine war for German development cooperation. Germany may work more intensively with other countries and international organisations to support a peaceful resolution of the conflict and mitigate the impacts of the war on development cooperation.

Overall, the Ukraine war has posed new challenges to German development cooperation and requires adjustments in priorities and measures to effectively respond to the needs of the affected regions. The long-term response could lead to a more comprehensive and coordinated strategy to promote peace, stability, and sustainable development not only in Europe but also globally. These adjustments are crucial to adequately address the challenges of the conflict and bring about long-term positive changes (Bliman 2024, 345–379).

Dynamics of German Development Cooperation: Continuous Adaptation to Changing Global Challenges

The periodisation of German state development cooperation illustrates its dynamic nature and its ability to adapt to changing global challenges. This development goes through various phases, which, however, cannot be strictly separated from each other but rather show a continuous adaptation and further development of strategies and priorities over time.

In the early phase of German development cooperation after the Second World War, the focus was on humanitarian aid and economic support for countries of the Global South. Germany focused on meeting basic needs such as food, medical care, and infrastructure to promote post-war reconstruction (Promberger 2010, 84–107).

In the following decades, the focus shifted to long-term development policy and sustainable development. Germany began to build long-term partnerships and invested more heavily in education systems, health infrastructure, agriculture, and economic promotion to address the structural causes of economic poverty and promote sustainable growth.

With the increase in global challenges such as climate change, migration, and security risks, German state development cooperation increasingly integrated these aspects into its strategies. Cross-sectoral approaches were developed to address not only acute problems but also the underlying causes of economic poverty and inequality.

Presently, innovative approaches and partnerships are crucial to deal with complex global challenges. Germany is working intensively with other countries, civil society, the private sector, and international organisations to achieve sustainable development goals and promote innovative solutions (Gieler and Nowak 2021, 301–322).

The flexibility and adaptability of German state development cooperation are crucial to effectively respond to the constantly changing global landscape. They enable the promotion of long-term development goals by addressing both present needs and preparing for future challenges. Through continuous adaptation and innovation, German state development cooperation can have a sustainable and positive impact on global development by contributing to a fairer and more stable world.

References

Bliman, A. (2024). Ukraine. In W. Gieler & M. Nowak (Eds.), Deutsche Entwicklungszusammenarbeit im Spannungsfeld der Außen- und Sicherheitspolitik. (Re-)konstruktionen – Internationale und Globale Studien (345–379). Wiesbaden.

Bundesministerium für wirtschaftliche Zusammenarbeit und Entwicklung. (2021). Entwicklungspolitischer Aktionsplan zur Gleichberechtigung der Geschlechter 2016–2020: Ein Rückblick. Retrieved from https://www.bmz.de/resource/blob/100930/bmz-rueckblick-gapii.pdf

Bundesministerium für wirtschaftliche Zusammenarbeit und Entwicklung. (2022, December 1). Pressemitteilung: Aktuelle Entwicklungen in der deutschen Digitalstrategie. Retrieved from https://www.bmz.de/de/aktuelles/aktuelle-meldungen/pressemitteilung-dezember-2022

Gieler, W. (2023). Reguliertes Chaos: (Re-)Konstruktionen zum westlichen Ethnozentrismus (2nd ed.). Bonn.

Gieler, W., & Nowak, M. (2021). Staatliche Entwicklungszusammenarbeit in Deutschland: Eine Bestandsaufnahme des BMZ 1961–2021. Wiesbaden.

Gieler, W., & Schwarz, M. (Eds.). (2020). Entwicklungszusammenarbeit im europäischen Vergleich: Eine grundlegende Einführung in die Politik ausgewählter Staaten (2nd ed.). Berlin.

Giessmann, H.-J. (2005). Die Anfänge der deutschen Entwicklungszusammenarbeit nach dem Zweiten Weltkrieg. In Frieden ist anders (123–145). Frankfurt.

Hentges, G. (2015). Die deutsche Entwicklungszusammenarbeit im Zeitalter der Globalisierung. Entwicklungspolitik, 25(4), 367–382.

Mair, J. (2017). Die Rolle der deutschen Entwicklungszusammenarbeit in der Agenda 2030 für nachhaltige Entwicklung. Österreichische Zeitschrift für Politikwissenschaft, 46 (2), 189–205.

Promberger, M. (2010). Die Rolle der Entwicklungshilfe in der Bonner Republik. Geschichte und Gesellschaft, 36 (1), 84–107.

Schmidt, J. (2020). Deutschlands Rolle in der globalen Entwicklungszusammenarbeit: Motive und Ziele im Wandel der Zeit. Internationale Politik, 75 (4), 45–62.

Schneckener, U. (2007). Die deutsche Entwicklungszusammenarbeit in den 1970er Jahren. WeltTrends, 54, 61–76.

Truman, H. S. (1949). Inaugural Address. Retrieved from https://www.presidency.ucsb.edu/documents/inaugural-address-6

Unmüssig, B. (1999). Die Ära der UN-Dekaden: Deutsche Entwicklungspolitik in den 1980er und 1990er Jahren. Zeitschrift für Politikwissenschaft, 9 (3), 321–339.

Chapter 2
Beginnings of (West) German Development Policy Between Continuity and Priorities

Wolfgang Gieler

Abstract An examination of the various development policy concepts at the beginning of state (West) German development policy is undertaken, with particular emphasis on the Gymnich theses, which have played a significant role in the development of this policy. In the course of the analysis, the transformation of state German development policy from a pure "development aid" to a more comprehensive "development cooperation" is thoroughly illuminated. Both the influences of the Gymnich theses and the development and implementation of various development policy concepts and strategies are critically examined. The political, economic and social influences that have shaped the development of (West) German development policy are taken into account. Overall, this in-depth analysis provides a comprehensive understanding of the evolution of state German development policy and highlights its significance in the international context.

Two statements, 26 years apart and made in completely different international contexts, which at first glance seem to have no direct connection to each other, determine the core of the following remarks. Heidemarie Wieczorek-Zeul, former Federal Minister for Economic Cooperation and Development, stated in her speech on the occasion of the 40th anniversary of the Federal Ministry for Economic Cooperation and Development (BMZ) in 2001: "Egon Bahr is also responsible for the 25 Gymnich theses, which became the basis of German development policy in June 1975. [Their] fields of action are still central to us today (…)" (Wieczorek-Zeul 2001).

W. Gieler (✉)
Sozialwissenschaften, Fachhochschule Dortmund, Dortmund, Nordrhein-Westfalen, Germany
e-mail: wolfgang.gieler@fh-dortmund.de

© The Author(s), under exclusive license to Springer Fachmedien Wiesbaden GmbH, part of Springer Nature 2024
W. Gieler, M. Nowak (eds.), *Understanding German Development Cooperation*, Contributions to Political Science, https://doi.org/10.1007/978-3-658-45596-5_2

Egon Bahr's Vision: A Bridge Connecting German Development Policy Across Decades

The 25 Gymnich theses were developed in 1975 by Egon Bahr, Federal Minister for Economic Cooperation between 1974 and 1976, in the run-up to the revision of the development policy concept of 1973 and formed the basic framework of the development policy concept of the Federal Government of 1975. The first of the theses reads among other things: "The principle of continuity and concentration also applies to development policy" (Bahr 1975 698). Bahr thus adopted the formula "continuity and concentration", which originally Helmut Schmidt used in his government declaration of 1974 as guideline for the future policy of the Federal Republic of Germany, and transferred this demand also into the framework of development policy.

The following article analyses the development line of federal German development policy against the background of international changes, in which context the 25 Gymnich theses were created. This is intended to show why the theses still largely hold true today and what achievements were made with them. What is the framework for action that was created with them, and how was the concept of continuity and concentration implemented within the Gymnich theses?

With the financial participation of the Federal Government in the expanded assistance programme of the United Nations, the beginning of federal German development policy is described in the scientific literature (BMZ 2020; Gieler 2008, 10). In addition, the Bundestag in 1956 for the first time allocated budget funds amounting to 50 million DM for development aid in the budget of the Foreign Office (Hofmeier 1982, 241). Development policy was a rather peripheral social issue at that time. Society was too much occupied with reconstruction, a furious economic upswing and the escalating East-West conflict. However, due to its strong export and raw material dependence, the Federal Republic also had to look at potential future markets. Thus, the Ministry of Economic Affairs (BMWi) faced the question of export orders, raw material security and new investment fields in order to secure long-term foreign trade. In this context, development aid was an excellent tool for the purpose of opening up and securing new international markets (Korff 1997, 4).

On the other hand, the Foreign Office was keen to instrumentalise development policy in the sense of the "Hallstein Doctrine" for German political purposes and in this way to assert the Federal Republic's sole representation claim against the developing countries. As a result, development aid was preferentially given to developing countries that refrained from diplomatic recognition of the GDR. In addition, development aid was preferentially given to rather Western-oriented states of the Third World against the backdrop of the East-West conflict. In this way, the strategy of the watering can principle was established.

With this principle of distributing financial and technical aid, as many states as possible were to be reached in order to prevent the spread of communism to non-aligned territory (Nuscheler 1977, 327; Gieler 1999). "Development policy was and is a policy of interest dependent on overarching goals. The 'aid to the underdeveloped countries' was initially a misbirth of the Cold War" (Nuscheler 2005, 78).

With the decolonisation that progressed particularly rapidly in the 1960s, the landscape of states on the political world map changed significantly. Another consequence was, among other things, that the composition in the United Nations increasingly changed in favour of the developing countries, which also allowed the development problem itself to move more into the centre. The growing influence of developing countries within the UN was further amplified by their increased selforganization. Mergers such as the "Movement of Non-Aligned States" founded in 1961 or the "Group of 77" from 1964 spoke with one voice to the outside world and thus gave their demands much more emphasis (Ihne and Wilhelm 2006, 10).

In 1961, the United Nations General Assembly, on the initiative of the Kennedy administration, proclaimed the first development decade. The main goals were to promote the economic growth of the developing countries through modernisation of existing structures and their integration into the world market. According to the principle of development through growth, it was believed that it would be possible to promote growth and development through capital inflows from outside. However, it fell into the assumption that underdevelopment was due solely to a lack of capital, and it also fell into the assumption that a so-called trickle-down effect would occur, namely, the belief that growth and modernisation would draw economically backward regions into their wake and "trickle down" to the economically poorest at the periphery (Nuscheler 2005, 78ff.).

The ongoing rise in global economic poverty was unavoidable. The Pearson Report of 1969, which was the first comprehensive analysis of two decades of development policy, revealed these findings and asserted that there is not only a 'crisis of development' but also a 'crisis of development aid itself, as a significant portion of bilateral development aid primarily aimed at securing short-term political or strategic advantages or promoting the exports of donor countries' (Nuscheler 2005, 78).

The Evolution of German Development Policy: From Fragmentation to Coordination

In German development policy, there were initially no uniform framework conditions. Development policy was carried out under the primarily German political guidelines of the Foreign Office and the Federal Ministry of Economics. The increasing pressure from the United States on the Federal Republic to contribute significantly more financially to the US development programme—the Alliance for Progress (annually between 3 and 4 billion DM)—which of course itself primarily followed global political, system-securing guidelines, required better coordination of German development aid measures (Spanger and Brock 1987, 280).

Development policy, embedded in a programme with defined priorities, should give way to spontaneous and ad hoc development aid, which the Federal Republic had pursued until then (Korff 1997, 4). In the autumn of 1961, the Federal Ministry for Economic Cooperation (BMZ) was founded. Under the first Federal Minister Walter Scheel, this newly created ministry was now to meet the growing volume of German aid services, as well as the desire for a bundling of development policy measures (Holtz 2006, 32).

Initially, however, few competencies were transferred to the BMZ. It had to assert itself alongside the already difficult position between the AA and the BMWi, with only a coordination function and the task of developing a development policy programme. Thus, financial and technical aids were primarily handled in cooperation between the BMWi and the Kreditanstalt für Wiederaufbau (KfW) (Korff 1997, 3ff.). The AA set the framework conditions, always in the context of the Hallstein Doctrine. The work of the BMZ therefore had to primarily orient itself towards foreign, German and economic policy interests.

German development policy was understood until 1968 as "(...) an instrument of short- and long-term system security and crisis regulation (...) as an export-promoting and economic stabilising instrument (...)" (Nuscheler 1977, 327ff.). Especially against the background of the first economic crisis in 1965/1966, development policy was communicated to the public based on economic self-interest, which saw in development aid measures rather billion-dollar graves than forward-looking investment. However, precisely through the institutionalisation of development policy in the tension field between the AA and the BMWi, there was the opportunity to look beyond foreign and economic policy motives. This also became necessary as doubts about the concept of development through growth arose with the Pearson Report.

Shifting Priorities: The Transformation of German Development Policy Under Erhard Eppler

With development minister Erhard Eppler (1968–1974), German development aid received new accents. On the one hand, economic relations with the countries of the Third World became more important, not least because of the economic and business cycle crisis within the Federal Republic. The increasing North-South disputes over global economic issues also contributed to this (Nuscheler 1977, 290). On the other hand, the prospects of being able to enforce the Federal Republic's sole representation claim became increasingly gloomy. Towards the end of the 1960s, the number of states that established diplomatic relations with the GDR despite threats from the Foreign Office increased successively. In 1969/1970 alone, 12 states established diplomatic relations with the GDR. Under threat from the Foreign Office, for example, Cambodia broke off relations with the FRG and all ongoing development projects of its own accord. A comprehensive analysis is provided by Spanger and Bock (1987, 290ff.).

Thus, the social-liberal coalition, as part of its Eastern policy (Eastern treaties), with the Basic Treaty between the GDR and the Federal Republic of 1972 and the associated, among other things, burial of the Hallstein Doctrine, advanced German development policy by giving it significantly more room for manoeuvre. Willy Brandt promised in his government declaration of 1969 to contribute to a common strategy of development, which was ultimately realised with the first development policy concept of the Federal Government of 1971 (Hein 2006, 193ff.).

Against the background of the findings of the Pearson Report, Eppler interpreted development policy as international social and peace policy and put the needs of the developing countries more in the foreground (Korff 1997, 5). In the sense of a long-term overcoming of underdevelopment and in the sense of enabling self-help, longer-term and country-specific aid programmes were to be created. The development aid granted to more than 100 states should, in view of scarce resources, be reduced to less than 30. States reduced, so that—in stark contrast to the scattergun approach—resources are sensibly bundled and genuine, lasting partnerships are formed (Hein 2006, 253). Eppler explained in his general formula for development policy: "Development policy is an approach to global domestic policy. It does the most immediate thing in a revolutionary world situation. Development policy aims for peace. It proves and mobilises hope" (SPD 1968/69, 152). This moved the trend initially away from a more pragmatically interpreted development policy of short-term self-interests to a development policy increasingly based on humanitarian grounds (Morgenschweiß 2006, 7).

At the centre of the second development policy decade was the concept of the basic needs strategy. Development policy no longer aimed solely at overcoming underdevelopment but was characterised by the fight against economic poverty. The focus was primarily on basic provision through rural development and self-help, the political and economic participation of people and the guarantee of human rights. As early as 1970, the 0.7% target was adopted with UN Resolution 2626, after the donor countries committed to continuously increase their public services for development aid (Official Development Assistance, ODA) to 0.7% of GNP (Ihne and Wilhelm 2006, 10).

By the time of the speech by World Bank President Robert McNamara in 1973 in Nairobi, which painted a bleak picture of the catastrophic conditions, mass impoverishment and dramatic need of people in the Third World, it was clear that the most urgent development policy goal could only be the fight against mass poverty (Nuscheler 2005, 79). This picture showed that the concept of development through growth had failed. Moreover, it was necessary to finally abandon the belief in a one-sided dependence of the developing countries on the industrialised countries.

With the oil crisis of 1973, the mutual dependence, the interdependence between industrialised and developing countries, became apparent. The increase in oil prices and the supply boycotts against the backdrop of the escalating Middle East conflict against the United States and some EEC countries by OPEC clearly showed that developing countries, when they act in unison, represent a large political and economic power factor that can shake the established international political and economic system more than just a little.

Towards Equitable Development: The Changing Landscape of Global Economic Relations

Thus, the demands for a reorganisation of the world economy made by the countries of the Third World since the beginning of the 1970s gradually found a hearing at international conferences (Tetzlaff 1982, 65ff.). In 1974, these demands were met by the adoption of Resolution 3281, the Charter of Economic Rights and Duties of States by the 29th UN General Assembly and the Declaration on the Establishment of a New World Economic Order at the UN Conference on Raw Materials and Energy (Ihne and Wilhelm 2006, 10).

The intention to promote the establishment of a new world economic order aimed primarily at a fair balance of interests between industrialised and developing countries and an interdependent partnership (Kühnhardt 1980, 13). What appeared incompatible with the interests of the industrial nations was the intention of the developing countries to replace a dirigiste or centrally led world economic system with the prevailing free trade system operating according to market economic principles, in order to escape, among other things, the role of the cheap raw material supplier, to act as an equal trading partner who not only offers markets but can also export at fair prices, in order to ultimately satisfy its basic needs.

However, numerous conferences also made it clear that there is awareness in the industrialised countries that the demands of the developing countries were justified. The Lome Agreement of 1975 between the states of the African, Caribbean and the Pacific region (ACP states) and the EC was a first step in this context. Essentially, economic and technical assistance, general trade preferences, improved market access conditions and mechanisms for stabilising raw material export revenues were granted to the ACP states, and a development fund was set up to finance infrastructure, education and health projects (Mair 1999). Also at the UNCTAD conferences, which have been held every 4 years since 1964, particularly at the conference in Nairobi in 1976, the developing countries were able to achieve successes, managing to push through demands for an integrated raw material programme and the associated joint fund for financing raw material balancing warehouses, which was intended to balance and stabilise fluctuating raw material prices at the expense of the exporting countries (Betz 1982, 187ff.).

There was disagreement about the creation of a new world economic order, especially on the part of the industrialised nations, particularly about the scope and intensity of the reforms (Schloz 1979, 176ff.). Thus, alongside the United States, the Federal Government was initially immovable when it came to shaking the foundations of the so-called "free" world economy. As the "guardian of the market economy", it was convinced that "(…) the growth of the developing countries is inextricably linked with that of the industrialised countries. (…) The necessary further development of international economic relations must therefore not invalidate their market economic structures (…)" (Bundesregierung 1975, 2). What was overlooked was that the principle of the market economy, on the principles of which the

Federal Republic was able to experience its enormous economic upswing after the Second World War, always also has a downside to the prosperity medal.

With the development policy concept of the Federal Republic of 1971, a uniform framework for German development policy was created for the first time, which contains an extensive catalogue of guiding principles. The concept is based on the strategy for the second development decade proclaimed by the United Nations in 1970, in whose principles development policy is seen as an instrument of peace-keeping, whose main task, in the sense of the basic needs strategy, lies among other things in securing food production and creating educational opportunities and jobs in the Third World.

The experiences and insights of the first development decade have been incorporated into the concept, which tends to mean a departure from the development aid practice of the past decade. This includes, among other things, the recognition of the failure of the principle of development through growth and the insight that development policy must not be misused as an instrument of political self-interest. The latter is explicitly addressed in point 2, but also in point 3, as an increased effort for multilateral aid inevitably leads to a reduction in bilateral aid, which is most susceptible to the suspicion of enforcing one's own interests.

> [1] Development policy efforts should primarily serve social progress in the countries of the Third World; economic growth alone does not guarantee progress for the majority of the people affected.
>
> [2] Development policy must not be an instrument for achieving short-term foreign policy goals.
>
> [3] A larger proportion of the Federal Republic's development aid than before should go to multilateral organisations, such as the United Nations Development Programme (…) (SPD 1970–72, 49ff.).

Furthermore, the concept provides for a focus in the context of technical and financial cooperation. Instead of a multitude of isolated individual projects, country-specific and internationally coordinated aid programmes should be introduced, which are oriented towards the conditions and objectives of the individual developing country. Priorities include, among others, combating unemployment and underemployment, improving structures in rural regions and immediate aid to improve living conditions. Within the EC, the Federal Government wants to have a stronger influence on their trade policy, among other things, with the aim of establishing general trade preferences for developing countries (BMZ 1971, 263ff.).

In principle, the concept aims for a qualitative and quantitative improvement of development aid, which is reflected in the easing of credit conditions for capital aid, the increase of multilateral aid, a reduction in the proportion of tied credits, the quantitative and qualitative expansion of personnel aid and increased cooperation with private aid organisations (points C3, C4 in BMZ 1971, S269ff.).

The Gymnich Theses and the Shift Towards Integrated Economic Diplomacy

In the updated development policy concept of 1973, the Federal Government largely remained true to its principles. However, against the background of the Third World Trade and Development Conference and the European Summit Conference 1972, some elements had to be added or supplemented. As part of the demands for a new world economic order, the developing countries increasingly asserted their claims for a reorganisation of international trade and monetary policy, which received all the more attention in view of the emerging world economic crisis. The main issues were demands such as the regulation of commodity and goods markets through internationally financed commodity stocks, the problem of debt restructuring and cancellation, the opening of the markets *of* industrialised countries for goods from developing countries, the questions of a redesign of international monetary policy, etc. (Schloz 1979, 184ff.).

The point of trade and monetary policy was included in the concept of 1973, announcing that the developing countries will be more intensively integrated into the international division of labour by involving them more intensively in trade negotiations than before, promoting foreign trade, reducing trade barriers and improving tariff preferences (BMZ 1973, 27ff.). Furthermore, the point of European development policy has been expanded. The Federal Government declares the European Community, the main trading partner of the Third World, to be obliged to integrate developing countries as equal trading partners into world trade. The Federal Government "(...) will use its policy to ensure that the European Community takes into account the interests of all developing countries in shaping its common trade and raw materials policy, regional, industrial, agricultural, and monetary policy" (BMZ 1973, 25).

Egon Bahr wrote in an article in the magazine *Außenpolitik* in the context of the revision of the development policy concept of 1973: "Development policy is neither an appendage nor a luxury, but claims increasing attention in the interest of the future of our country" (Bahr 1975, 316). On the one hand, the quote makes clear that development policy is in a field of tension between domestic political legitimation and foreign policy instrumentalisation. On the other hand, it unmistakably shows in which direction German development policy is heading in the future.

Chancellor Helmut Schmidt, who in Egon Bahr's memories showed little interest in the problems of the Third World (Bahr 1996, 465; Gieler 2008, 57–69), dismissed Bahr in 1974 to the office of the Federal Minister for Economic Cooperation with the words: "Do what you think is right, but as little trouble as possible" (Bahr 1996, 466). This initially confirms the low importance that Schmitt attached to development policy. But it also shows what delicate tasks Bahr now faced. Various factors determined Bahr's work. On the one hand, development policy had little lobby in the public as well as in the government. His predecessor Eppler was completely isolated in the cabinet at the end (Hein 2006, 294).

On the other hand, Bahr saw himself in addition to his office as minister domestically in the mediator position between Brandt as party chairman and Schmitt as chancellor. Both did not have the best relationship to each other. Only Brandt was able to convince Bahr to accept the position of minister. Bahr was known for his diplomatic skill and ultimately, in tandem with Brandt, was responsible for the hitherto successful détente policy in the East-West conflict. Thus, accepting the office would "(…) externally prove continuity and (…) internally reduce or prevent friction between the party and the government" (Bahr 1996, 466).

The third factor was the influence of the Foreign Office on development policy. Bahr tried to limit the geographical distribution of aid. Thus, development policy engagement should focus particularly on the Mediterranean countries and Africa while being diluted in Asia and Latin America (Sigrist 2005, 1041). Bahr justified the focus on Africa with the security policy argument and the necessary differentiation between developing countries in terms of their respective levels of development, as the economically poorest countries were to be found on the African continent. The continent is on Europe's doorstep. Moreover, it would be more sensible to direct the limited German resources towards Africa, where a much higher impact could be achieved. Furthermore, it seemed to him absurd to put money into an Indian budget that could finance a mature nuclear programme (Bahr 1996, 468).

On the other hand, the Foreign Office represents much more differentiated interests: "[-] Worldwide orientation of German development aid; as good relations as possible with all developing countries; development aid is a component and prerequisite of good relations; therefore, maintaining our development policy commitment in all continents and developing countries, at least as a presence programme (…). In all cases, it should be considered that a relatively minor increase brings much more political goodwill in the less considered developing countries than a corresponding increase in the so-called focus countries. The dilution of our (…) commitment in Asia and Latin America would run counter to the policy of the Foreign Office" (Sigrist 2005, 1042).

On 9 June 1975, Egon Bahr, since 1974 the new Federal Minister for Economic Cooperation, presented the Federal Cabinet with 25 theses for a revision of the development policy concept of 1973 at its retreat at Gymnich Castle. These, according to Bahr, should meet the international economic and political changes, the shifts in weight between North and South. New principles in German development policy are necessary to respond to the changed situation. One-sided dependencies of developing countries on industrialised countries, which became clear at the latest with the oil crisis at the end of 1973, no longer exist. In addition to the intensive interdependence of North and South, a sometimes extreme differentiation process has also begun among the developing countries themselves, to which Germany must adjust (Bahr 1975, 315).

The enormous increase in oil prices has hit hardest those states of the Third World that have no resources at all and have fallen into a cycle of debt and impoverishment that cannot be stopped without outside help. In contrast, there are the developing countries that, with their merger in OPEC, represent a new serious power factor in the international system. On the other hand, against this background, there is the difficulty for the Federal Republic to reconcile its raw material interests with its foreign and development policy. For this reason, development policy was no longer seen as a closed area with the adoption of the Gymnich theses but was integrated into trade, economic and foreign policy (Bahr 1975, 319).

The new conception of development policy is reflected, and this shows not least its importance, in thesis 2: "Development policy is part of the overall policy of the Federal Government; it will strive to achieve a balance between development policy requirements and our other interests to establish" (Bahr 1975a, 698). These "other" interests are highlighted in some of the following theses. In accordance with their increasing international political and economic importance, the OPEC states are intensively integrated into the Gymnich thesis catalogue.

In theses 7, 8, 9 and 10, these states, due to their enormous financial resources, are called upon to participate more intensively in the development policy work of the industrialised countries in the form of contributions to international institutions such as the International Monetary Fund (IMF) or the World Bank. In return, they are granted more voting rights within this framework (explicitly theses 7 and 8 in Bahr 1975a, 698). Furthermore, artificial interdependencies are sought with the OPEC states, which are not named, but become all too clear in the context of the global economic or oil crisis. The Federal Government also intends to support the development process of these countries in the context of building a capable infrastructure and industrial structure, with a particular focus on cooperation in the technical and scientific field, but also private services and general trade policy should be promoted (thesis 9 ibid., 698).

In this way, structures are created that make Germany an indispensable partner and ultimately secure exports and raw materials in the long term. In addition, Bahr's pragmatic idea of so-called triangular cooperation (thesis 10 in Bahr 1975a, 698) saves own financial resources, also promotes own exports and creates mutual dependencies. According to this idea, the OPEC states should primarily finance German know-how and technical aid for less affluent developing countries with their oil dollars (SPD 1973–1975, 20ff.).

This obvious emphasis on German, especially economic, self-interests is also evident in further theses. Thesis 20 is exemplary for the new integration of development policy into foreign and economic policy: "The Federal Government will endeavour to reconcile the interest in securing the raw material supply of the German economy with the interests of the developing countries in increasing their exports and expanding raw material processing" (Bahr 1975a, 699). At this point, only the economic aspect is addressed, thus emphasising the importance of economic self-interests once again, while the development policy issue does not find any consideration. A very similar tendency is revealed by thesis 21. "(…) with special consideration of the offer of the German economy (…)" (Bahr 1975a, 699), the expansion of technical cooperation is sought.

However, there are also elements with initially more selfless features, which, upon closer inspection, serve the legitimate German interest in reducing international tensions. In theses 14, 15 and 16, the Federal Government declares its intention that the countries most affected by the economic crisis will receive more favourable conditions within the framework of financial cooperation. The available resources will be used with a focus, with the share for the economically poorest of the poor to be further increased, the expansion of rural development to be further promoted and supply crises to be overcome with the help of food aid (Bahr 1975a, 699). On the other hand, thesis 4 announces the stagnation of multilateral aid (Bahr 1975a, 698).

Since the majority of the theses point to an increased focus on bi- but also trilateral cooperation with the developing countries, a stronger emphasis on West German self-interests can be demonstrated, which are long term in the context of German economic and trade policy such as raw material security, but also security policy aspects.

In the second revision of the development policy concept of 1975, the Gymnich theses have been integrated and have thus contributed to a significant renewal of the principles of German development policy. This is confirmed, initially still abstract, in the exchange of a few words, words of central importance. In the goals and principles of the 1973 concept, it still says: Development policy "(…) is not suitable as an instrument of short-term foreign policy considerations" (BMZ 1973, 11). However, in the 1975 concept, omitting this statement, it is pointed out: Development policy "(…) is oriented (…) towards long-term considerations" (Federal Government 1975, 57).

With the 1975 concept, the integration of German development policy into overall policy and thus its importance as an instrument of German policy is made clear by granting it, on the one hand, a certain independence in terms of its own instruments and methodology. On the other hand, however, it "requires (…) the complementation by measures in other areas of German policy. As part of the overall policy (…) it must therefore be coordinated with other objectives of the Federal Government" (Federal Government 1975, 58).

These goals can be seen, among other things, in the expansion of the paragraph on trade and monetary policy. "The increasing interdependence of the world economy requires closer cooperation between industrialised countries, raw material and other developing countries; it is in the primary interest of all to ensure and improve the functioning and performance of the world economy" (Federal Government 1975, 67). In addition, the Federal Government pursues the goal in international raw material policy to bring about more stable export revenues and to eliminate extreme price fluctuations in the interest of industrial and developing countries. "It also wants to contribute to a steady and sufficient supply of the economy with raw materials at reasonable prices" (Federal Government 1975, 68). In this context, a "(…) functioning international monetary system (…) is essential for both the industrial and developing countries as a prerequisite for successful economic policy" (Federal Government 1975, 68).

This makes it clear that, in addition to the strong emphasis on raw material security, it is also necessary to create or maintain stabilising conditions for the international world economy that flank and promote the economic growth of the Federal Republic. In addition, there is the intention developed with the 25 theses for increased cooperation with the rich OPEC countries in the area of increased cooperation in technical and scientific cooperation and further expansion of the infrastructure and industrial sector, as well as the also explained element of triangular cooperation, which increasingly points to an interest-oriented development program (Federal Government 1975, 65).

Although the increasing differentiation process among the developing countries themselves is taken into account and it is emphasised that, in contrast, differentiations in the conditions for capital aid are made, increased aid for the economically poorest states should be provided, and in the sense of the basic needs strategy the priority is given to measures to increase agricultural production. However, the 1975 concept primarily focuses on securing long-term self-interests.

Conclusion

The development policy of the Federal Republic of Germany has emerged and is embedded in a complex global context. International and national development policy cannot be viewed in isolation from the network of international policies and can hardly escape the associated instrumentalisation.

On the one hand, since the 1960s, the former colonial powers had the task of coming to terms with their past and providing development or reconstruction aid in a moral sense. On the other hand, political and economic conflicts at the international level influence the development policy of all states. The Federal Republic of Germany, whose German-German border was the demarcation line of the East-West conflict, whose territory would have been the staging area for the armies of the world in the event of a war outbreak, had an interest in this respect alone, to defuse international conflicts, but still showed loyalty to their Western allies.

Alongside this, there was a need to keep the economic upswing alive to avoid domestic tensions. As a country poor in raw materials, the German export economy depends on the resources of other countries; especially the so-called Third World countries were considered cheap raw material suppliers until the economic crisis of 1973. Until this point, development policy was pure development aid. With it, one could keep raw material suppliers on board and in an ideological sense containment policy against the communist Eastern Bloc.

The increasing cartelisation of the resource-rich countries of the Third World, the associated power shifts on the international stage, the worsening situation of the economically poorest resource-poor countries and the new awareness of the finiteness of resources demanded new strategies for security, economic and trade policy on an international level. The development line of West German development policy can be used to trace the reaction to the international changes. The most striking point was the development policy of short-term self-interest in the 1960s. Development policy was, in addition to the enforcement of economic interests, the instrument of crisis regulation and system security in the context of the Hallstein Doctrine.

In the 1970s, this strategy changed against the background of the new situation on an international level. West German development policy was caught between legitimacy, the trade, economic and foreign policy interests of Germany and the changes on an international level. Egon Bahr responded by embracing Helmut Schmidt's principle of 'continuity and concentration,' under which he formulated the Gymnich theses—a strategy rooted in long-term self-interest that laid the groundwork for the development of the concept of 'continuity and concentration.

The method of the watering can principle was replaced by the concentration on the countries that were of overall political relevance for the Federal Republic. In addition to the raw material exporters, the least developed countries are also included. The core of the strategy consisted in binding these countries in a partnership to the Federal Republic and thus in the context of global political and economic changes to secure in the long term. The transfer of scientific and technical knowhow to more developed developing countries played a role, as well as securing one's own supply, as well as the adapted aids for the so-called emerging countries and the least developed states.

The formula "continuity and concentration" in development policy has been realised in the sense of a long-term securing of one's own interests. The core was the 25 Gymnich theses, on the basis of which a reorientation of development policy has taken place. The content itself requires a more differentiated consideration. However, Egon Bahr has with the theses a groundbreaking strategy designed, which, as the former Federal Minister Heidemarie Wieczorek-Zeul confirmed, is still relevant today. Especially the focus on the least economically developed countries must be given more attention in the light of present global migration movements in one's own interest.

References

Bahr, E. (1974). Gemeinsame Verantwortung für die Entwicklungsprobleme [Erklärung von Bundesminister Bahr in Paris]. In Presse- und Informationsamt der Bundesregierung (Hrsg.), Bulletin Nr.125 (1263). Bonn.
Bahr, E. (1975). Die Thesen von Gymnich: Die Entwicklungspolitik der Bundesrepublik Deutschland. Außenpolitik. Zeitschrift für internationale Fragen, 26 (3), 315–321.
Bahr, E. (1975a). Politik der Zusammenarbeit mit den Entwicklungsländern. 25 Thesen von Gymnich. In Presse- und Informationsamt der Bundesregierung (Hrsg.), Bulletin Nr.75 (697–699). Bonn.
Bahr, E. (1996). Zu meiner Zeit. München.
Bellers, J. (2000). Innen- und außenpolitische Einflussfaktoren auf die Entwicklungspolitik der Bundesrepublik Deutschland. In Diskussionspapiere des Faches Politikwissenschaft: Rote Reihe (Nr. 72). Siegen.
Betz, J. (1982). Kooperation statt Konflikt? Die Position der Bundesrepublik auf den Nord-Süd-Konferenzen. In R. Steinweg (Hrsg.), Hilfe + Handel = Frieden? Die Bundesrepublik in der Dritten Welt (176–202). Frankfurt.
Bundesministerium für wirtschaftliche Zusammenarbeit (BMZ). (1971). Entwicklungspolitische Konzeption der Bundesrepublik Deutschland für die Zweite Entwicklungsdekade. In Presse- und Informationsamt der Bundesregierung (Hrsg.), Bulletin Nr. 25 (263–274). Bonn.

Bundesministerium für wirtschaftliche Zusammenarbeit (BMZ) (Hrsg.). (1973). Die Entwicklungspolitische Konzeption der Bundesrepublik Deutschland und die Internationale Strategie für die Zweite Entwicklungsdekade (2nd ed.). Bonn.

Bundesministerium für wirtschaftliche Zusammenarbeit und Entwicklung (BMZ). (2020). Die Geschichte des Ministeriums. Retrieved from http://www.bmz.de/de/ministerium/geschichte/index.html#t2 (Accessed: December 14, 2023).

Bundesregierung. (1975). Entwicklungspolitische Konzeption der Bundesrepublik Deutschland 1975. In Unterrichtung durch die Bundesregierung, Dritter Bericht zur Entwicklungspolitik der Bundesregierung, Deutscher Bundestag, 8. Wahlperiode, Drucksache 8/1185. Retrieved from http://dip.bundestag.de/cgi-bin/getdokg?a=F+SQ='VT+BT+Drs+08/118 5'+and+T=X&b=1199098706-3960&c=/usr7/goldop&d=www.dia.bt/DIA&e=/bt_ st3kad&k=1998&m=2002&n=08 (Accessed: January 4, 2024).

Eppler, E. (1981). Wege aus der Gefahr. Hamburg.

Gieler, W. (1999). Die Entwicklungspolitik der Bundesrepublik Deutschland und der Deutschen Demokratischen Republik im Vergleich. In Diskussionspapiere des Faches Politikwissenschaft (Nr. 21). Siegen.

Gieler, W. (Hrsg.). (2008). Deutsche Entwicklungsminister von 1960–2008. Biographie, Konzeptionen und Einfluss auf nationale und internationale Entwicklungspolitik. Bonn.

Hein, B. (2006). Die Westdeutschen und die Dritte Welt, Entwicklungspolitik und Entwicklungsdienste zwischen Reform und Revolte 1959–1974. Oldenburg.

Hofmeier, R. (1982). Bonner Entwicklungspolitik: Grundlinien und Rahmenbedingungen. In R. Steinweg (Hrsg.), Hilfe + Handel = Frieden? Die Bundesrepublik in der Dritten Welt (240–267). Frankfurt.

Holtz, U. (2006). Abschied von der Gießkanne. Stationen aus 50 Jahren deutscher Entwicklungspolitik. Entwicklungspolitik Information Nord-Süd, No. 23–24, 32–36.

Ihne, H., & Wilhelm, J. (2006). Grundlagen der Entwicklungspolitik. In H. Ihne & J. Wilhelm (Eds.), Einführung in die Entwicklungspolitik (5–12). Hamburg.

Korff, R. (1997). Der Stellenwert der Entwicklungspolitik in der Bundesrepublik Deutschland. Working Paper der Universität Bielefeld, Fakultät für Soziologie, Forschungsschwerpunkt Entwicklungssoziologie (273). Bielefeld.

Kühnhardt, L. (1980). Die deutschen Parteien und die Entwicklungspolitik. Niedersächsische Landeszentrale für Politische Bildung (Hrsg.). Hannover.

Mair, S. (1999). Afrikapolitik der Europäischen Union. Informationen zur politischen Bildung, 264, 53–55.

Morgenschweiß, J. (2006). Traditionen sozialdemokratischer Entwicklungspolitik. Überblick über die Geschichte der Kolonial- und Entwicklungspolitik der SPD. In J. Bellers, C. R. Köster, J. Morgenschweiß, & J. Steinmetz (Eds.), Bundesdeutsche Entwicklungspolitik in der Ära Schmidt. Erster Bericht aus einem Forschungsprojekt an der Universität Siegen (4–9).

Nuscheler, F. (1977). Partnerschaft oder Ausbeutung? Die Entwicklungspolitik der sozial-liberalen Koalition. In F. Grube & G. Richter (Eds.), Der SPD-Staat (324–349). München.

Nuscheler, F. (2005). Entwicklungspolitik: Eine grundlegende Einführung in die zentralen entwicklungspolitischen Themenfelder Globalisierung, Staatsversagen, Hunger, Bevölkerung, Wirtschaft und Umwelt. Bonn.

Schloz, R. (1979). Deutsche Entwicklungspolitik: Eine Bilanz nach 25 Jahren. Geschichte und Staat (Bd. 228/229). München/Wien.

Sigrist, H. (2005). Äußerungen von Bahr zur künftigen Entwicklungspolitik der Bundesregierung. In Akten zur Auswärtigen Politik der Bundesrepublik Deutschland 1974 (Bd. 2: 1. Juli bis 31. Dezember 1974) (1040–1043). München.

Sozialdemokratische Partei Deutschlands (SPD). (1968/69). Jahrbuch der Sozialdemokratischen Partei Deutschlands 1968/1969. Bonn.

Sozialdemokratische Partei Deutschlands (SPD). (1970–72). Jahrbuch der Sozialdemokratischen Partei Deutschlands 1970–1972. Bonn.

Sozialdemokratische Partei Deutschlands (SPD). (1973–1975). Jahrbuch der Sozialdemokratischen Partei Deutschlands 1973–1975. Bonn.

Spanger, H.-J., & Brock, L. (1987). Die beiden deutschen Staaten in der Dritten Welt: Die Entwicklungspolitik der DDR- eine Herausforderung für die Bundesrepublik Deutschland? Opladen.

Tetzlaff, R. (1982). Die Dritte-Welt-Politik der Bundesrepublik Deutschland zwischen Friedensrhetorik und Realpolitik. Eine Einführung mit politischen Empfehlungen. In R. Steinweg (Ed.), Hilfe + Handel = Frieden? Die Bundesrepublik in der Dritten Welt (49–108). Frankfurt.

Uschner, M. (1992). Egon Bahr und seine Wirkung auf uns. In D. S. Lutz (Ed.), Das Undenkbare denken. Festschrift für Egon Bahr zum siebzigsten Geburtstag (73–76). Baden-Baden.

Vogtmeier, A. (1996). Egon Bahr und die deutsche Frage: Zur Entwicklung der sozialdemokratischen Ost- und Deutschlandpolitik von Kriegsende bis zur Vereinigung. Bonn.

Wieczorek-Zeul, H. (2001). 40 Jahre deutsche Entwicklungszusammenarbeit [Rede der Bundesministerin für wirtschaftliche Zusammenarbeit und Entwicklung anlässlich des Festaktes zum 40-jährigen Bestehen des Bundesministeriums für wirtschaftliche Zusammenarbeit und Entwicklung]. Retrieved from http://www.bmz.de/de/presse/reden/ministerin/07112001.html

Chapter 3
State Development Policy in German-German Comparison: FRG and GDR

Wolfgang Gieler

Abstract The development policy of the FRG (Federal Republic of Germany) and the GDR (German Democratic Republic) during the Cold War showed clear differences in their approaches and symbolisms. The GDR placed great emphasis on "socialist fraternal aid", especially towards other communist countries of the CMEA. This support emphasised solidarity and cohesion within the Eastern Bloc and strengthened the geopolitical position of the GDR. In contrast, the FRG pursued an independent development policy, closely linked to its foreign policy. The establishment of the independent Ministry for Economic Cooperation and Development (BMZ) demonstrated the strategic intention to establish development aid as an independent policy field and to pursue the development policy objectives of the FRG. These different approaches reflect the political, ideological and geopolitical realities of the Cold War. While the GDR viewed its aid as part of an ideological alliance in the Eastern Bloc, the FRG pursued a development policy strategy to strengthen its position in the West.

Paradigms and Strategies

The development policy of the former GDR (German Democratic Republic) and the FRG (Federal Republic of Germany) during the Cold War can be clearly compared and analysed in their approaches and symbolisms. The GDR pursued a specific form of development policy, heavily influenced by its socialist ideology. A central element was the idea of "socialist fraternal aid", especially towards other communist countries of the CMEA (Council for Mutual Economic Assistance). The support provided by the GDR in the form of development aid and economic cooperation was seen as an expression of solidarity and cohesion between the socialist states.

W. Gieler (✉)
Sozialwissenschaften, Fachhochschule Dortmund, Dortmund, Nordrhein-Westfalen, Germany
e-mail: wolfgang.gieler@fh-dortmund.de

© The Author(s), under exclusive license to Springer Fachmedien Wiesbaden GmbH, part of Springer Nature 2024
W. Gieler, M. Nowak (eds.), *Understanding German Development Cooperation*, Contributions to Political Science, https://doi.org/10.1007/978-3-658-45596-5_3

This had a strong symbolic meaning and also served the geopolitical positioning of the GDR within the Eastern Bloc.

In contrast, the FRG pursued an independent development policy, closely linked to its foreign policy. The Federal Republic established an independent Ministry for Economic Cooperation and Development (BMZ) in 1961, which was specifically responsible for development policy matters. This reflected the intention to establish development aid as an independent policy field and to strategically pursue the development policy objectives of the FRG. The FRG also aimed to strengthen its position as a democratic and economically strong country in the West and relied on development policy measures as a tool of foreign policy.

The two German states thus pursued different paradigms and strategies in their development policy. While the GDR viewed its aid as part of an ideological alliance within the Eastern Bloc and used it as a means to strengthen its own position within this alliance, the FRG pursued a development policy strategy more closely linked to its own foreign policy profile and the goal of positioning in the West. These differences reflected the political, ideological and geopolitical realities of the Cold War and shaped the development policy of the two German states during this time.

In the 1950s, both the Federal Republic of Germany (FRG) and the German Democratic Republic (GDR) began their development policy engagement. Among the first significant projects were training and further education programmes for specialists and executives from Africa, Asia and Latin America. A distinctive feature of these programmes was that they were not conducted in the so-called developing countries themselves but in the FRG and the GDR. In addition to the development policy objectives, both Bonn and East Berlin pursued their own economic and foreign policy interests with these education programmes (Richter 2019, 245ff).

Both German states aimed to secure political ties with the cooperating governments and the specialists and executives engaged in the process. In this way, they hoped to gain allies in the East-West confrontation for their respective camps. Foreign economic motives also played a crucial role for both states. Thus, the FRG and the GDR appeared from the beginning as competitors on the international stage in their new development policy task against each other (Otto 2018).

The Development Policy of the Federal Republic of Germany

After the Second World War, a development began that had not previously taken place, with the gradual dissolution of the former colonial empires. The release of the former colonies into independence did not initially lead to an independent development of these countries. They were neither economically nor politically in the position to compete with the established states, whether colonial powers or not.

In view of this situation, these countries under the leadership of India (Nehru), Indonesia (Sukarno) and Egypt (Nasser) tried to find a common way out at the conferences of Bandung 1955 and Belgrade 1961 by initiating the movement of the "non-aligned" countries. They sought a 'third way' between capitalism and socialism, with the goal of overcoming economic dependence and exploitation, as well as reducing or eliminating the political patronage of the new states and their integration into the East-West divide (Spanger and Brock 1987, 23).

In the early 1950s, the economically developed industrial nations, especially the USA, had no clear ideas or concepts for a development policy (Galbraith 1980, 24 f.). The Federal Republic of Germany was in this decade after its foundation mainly concerned with the reconstruction of the destroyed country and the integration of over ten million refugees from the Eastern territories. A German development policy only began very reluctantly and more at the urging of the USA, who in view of the escalating East-West contrast demanded a division of the defence burdens and a "containment policy in the Third World against the Soviet Union" (Simon 1981, 4).

In the 1950s and 1960s, the development policy of the Federal Government served as an instrument of the "non-recognition policy" towards the GDR. The Hallstein Doctrine therefore directed at least until the end of the 1960s the fortunes in this area. Before the establishment of the "Federal Ministry for Economic Cooperation" (BMZ) in the year 1961, the Foreign Office, the Ministry of Agriculture, the Ministry of Economics and the Information and Press Office of the Federal Government were mainly active in development policy. Especially the Foreign Office took the lead, as it was primarily about implementing German foreign policy objectives. A diplomatic recognition of the GDR by the newly emerged developing countries should be prevented at all costs. Thus, development policy at this time was not yet established as an independent policy (Buro 1975, 331 f.).

In March 1956, the first development policy promotion measure was initiated in the federal budget at the initiative of the Bundestag and at the request of the SPD parliamentary group (Bodemer 1974, 30). In the budget 50 million DM was provided "to strengthen the relations of the Federal Republic with the developing countries, especially in the cases, where the granting of economic aid does not directly serve the interest of German export promotion" (Bodemer 1974, 31). This first official development policy measure was primarily aimed at promoting exports.

Despite the first officially listed development measure in the budget in 1956, the activities of the Federal Government in the field of development policy go back to the year 1952. At this time, funds from the Marshall Plan were made available to the United Nations for their technical assistance programme (Bodemer 1974, 29). In the 1950s and 1960s, the Federal Republic of Germany primarily pursued a strategy that relied on private sector engagement and was supported by Federal Government guarantees. The public funds for development policy amounted to about 3.7 billion DM until 1960. In 1961, private investments amounted to only about 926 million DM, including direct investments, security investments, export credits and other loans. By 1969, these investments had risen to around 4.466 billion DM (Buro 1975, 330).

During the first development decade of the United Nations and the USA, the Federal Republic of Germany actively sought to promote industrial growth in developing countries. A central aspect of this strategy was the provision of capital aid, as the accumulation of capital for industrial investments was seen as a crucial prerequisite for economic growth (Simon 1981, 4). It was hoped that such economic growth would increase the per capita income of the population in developing countries and thus make them less susceptible to the "socialist temptations" of the Eastern Bloc.

The Federal Government not only had the goal of diplomatic recognition in mind but also actively sought to prevent an upgrade of the German Democratic Republic (GDR) in the countries of the so-called Third World. Despite these efforts, the GDR achieved remarkable successes in numerous developing countries during the decolonisation phase in the 1960s. This was particularly the case through the establishment and expansion of bilateral relations with the GDR in the areas of trade, sport, cultural exchange and the establishment of consulates. In the face of these successes, the policy of the Federal Republic of Germany increasingly took on the character of a retreat (Spanger and Brock 1987, 286–290).

The linking of development policy with the claim to sole representation led—in addition to the different competencies and priorities of the ministries involved—mainly to problems of the distribution of development policy funds. It was noticeable that the Foreign Office, for example, applied for around half a billion DM in special funds for Ghana and Indonesia, as well as for the Arab states in 1965, so that "friendly governments" could be encouraged in their friendly attitudes towards the FRG and other governments could be preserved from the "Egyptian disease" (Spanger and Brock 1987) in the form of a rapprochement with the GDR.

At its core, these efforts were aimed at the Non-Aligned Movement, where it was becoming apparent that an increasing number of so-called Third World countries could turn to the thesis of two German states.

> German aid [...] seemed to have the ambition to leave no country out. However, giving little to many is a less successful recipe. Although the German Bundestag had unanimously held the view that German development aid should be granted without conditions, this opinion did not prevail in administrative practice for a long time. Aid was given according to good behaviour criteria and not according to the absorption capacity of each individual country. It was inevitable that this policy would not be consistently successful (Sohn 1973, 14).

Only towards the end of the 1960s did German development policy take an independent direction and free itself from the tutelage of the Foreign Office and the Ministry of Economics. This was certainly also connected with the gradual crumbling of the rigid Hallstein Doctrine policy. Countries like Cuba, Algeria, Indonesia, Egypt and India took different paths in the 1960s and were no longer necessarily to be "well behaved" in the sense of the Hallstein Doctrine with the threat of withdrawal of development policy funds. In the long term, the foreign policy of the Federal Republic could not use development policy as a means of discipline. This had to lead in the long term to a political dead end in the sense of a "reversal of the Hallstein Doctrine". This topic became significant in May 1969 when Cambodia formally recognized the GDR, leading the Bonn coalition to distance itself through a rather vague foundational declaration. Following this, the social-liberal coalition redirected development policy with the introduction of its Eastern policy (Bodemer 1974, 136).

The development policy of the Federal Republic of Germany until the end of the 1960s can be traced back to three essential levels:

1. Promotion of individual projects and capital aid: The Federal Republic committed itself by supporting specific development projects and providing capital aid to promote industrial growth in developing countries.
2. Subordination to foreign policy with the premises of the Hallstein Doctrine: Due to the Hallstein Doctrine, development policy was integrated into foreign policy, which made the development of regional and country-specific concepts difficult.
3. Collection of important experiences in the Third World to promote economic expansion, securing raw material supplies and participation in international development aid bodies: The Federal Republic actively sought to gain experience in the Third World to support its economic expansion, secure access to raw materials and expand its influence in international development aid bodies (Buro 1975, 331 f.).

In the second phase of West German development policy, which essentially coincides with the second development decade of the United Nations, the social-liberal coalition abandoned the path of exchanging raw materials for industrial products. The new Development Minister Eppler formulated the new concept, which is based on an international division of labour, to bring the so-called Third World countries up to the standard of economically developed countries: "The benefit of the global economic division of labour is greatest in trade between industrialised countries. The following applies: the further industrialisation progresses in developing countries, the more opportunities for expanding trade, the more benefits for all participants from the global economic division of labour. This is particularly important for the Federal Republic of Germany, as a significant part of its social product is created through foreign economic relations" (Eppler 1971, 98 f.).

With this idea, the so-called developing countries should be enabled to break free from their dependence on industrialised countries. According to this thesis, it was about reducing the then already emerging heavy debt of developing countries. With the processing of their raw materials at an initially low level, these countries could gradually be included in fair international commodity exchange.

The gradual dismantling of the Hallstein Doctrine by the social-liberal coalition also brought about a reorientation of development policy. It was no longer seen as an "instrument of short-term foreign policy considerations", and the partner countries should not have "political as well as social and economic policy ideas" of the Federal Republic imposed on them (Simon 1981, 7). An indication of the redesign of development policy is the reorganisation of the BMZ from 1969. The ministry was given responsibility for planning capital aid as well as responsibility for projects in the technical and agricultural sectors and projects in the field of mass media (Buro 1975, 33).

With the détente policy at the beginning of the 1970s, the debate about a new order of the world economy, the expansion of the North-South debate and the oil crisis of 1973/1974, there was an "economisation of international relations" (Spanger and Brock 1987, 298). The oil crisis in particular had shown the vulnerability of industrial nations in the supply of raw materials. As a consequence, the Federal Government, led by the new Development Minister Egon Bahr, formulated its development policy concept anew in 1975 in the so-called Theses of Gymnich (Gieler 2010, 24).

These theses demanded for the Federal Republic within the framework of development policy the assurance of raw material supply to ensure economic growth. In addition, the "basic needs strategy", as formulated by the then President of the World Bank, Robert McNamara, in 1973, was included in the concept. It had been shown in the first development decade of the 1960s that the development of the so-called Third World countries could not automatically be created by expanding trade. Rather, alongside the growth strategy, the provision of basic needs for the economically poorest should now be ensured. These basic needs were to be activated by the self-help capability of the economically poor.

This gave increased attention to rural areas. However, this concept was not entirely new, as the so-called Green Revolution had already been propagated in the 1960s. It focused on the development of agriculture to increase production and self-sufficiency of the population. The discussion about agrarian reform was driven by the Chinese Revolution, the victory of the Cuban Revolution and experiments in numerous other countries. The basic problems lay primarily in the dilemma of creating additional jobs in agriculture for the growing population, securing the supply of these products and, on the other hand, earning the necessary foreign exchange for the development of their own national economy.

Thus, the German development policy in this phase in the 1970s can be divided into four areas:

1. Securing food supply.
2. Building an infrastructure.
3. Creating production capacities, which should form the basis of the new division of labour in underdeveloped countries.
4. Changing the production structure in industrialised countries (Buro 1975, 36).

However, the last area could no longer be enforced by the Federal Republic alone, as the advancing integration in the European Community did not allow this. Nevertheless, the Federal Republic increased the import of semifinished and finished goods from so-called Third World countries from 11 to 20 billion DM between 1976 and 1981 and even had a foreign trade deficit of one billion DM with non-OPEC developing countries in 1982 (Heimpel 1983, 4).

A new phase of the Federal Republic's development policy can be set with the end of the 1970s and at the latest with the beginning of the Christian-liberal coalition of the turnaround in 1982. However, new approaches were already emerging from the mid-1970s. A purely growth-oriented development left the question of human rights out of consideration. Influenced by their partner countries, the churches, in particular, and the CDU/CSU opposition in 1976 demanded a development policy that should serve to promote liberal, socially just infrastructures. All parliamentary parties joined this in a joint declaration in 1977, which demanded respect for human rights in developing countries. The new strategy now saw the implementation of democracy as a prerequisite for development, whereas before it was "democratisation through economic development" (Simon 1981, 10ff).

The hardening of the East-West opposition from the mid-1970s and the policy of the Reagan administration also made development policy in the Federal Republic more of a tool of foreign and security policy again. The direct invasion of Afghanistan in 1978/1979 by Soviet troops and the wars in Ethiopia, Angola and Mozambique with more or less direct military support from Eastern Bloc states eventually led to a renewed containment policy (neo-containment) also in the developing countries (Heimpel 1983, 4).

The new government of the turning point 1982/1983 placed development policy more under the economic self-interests of the Federal Republic and the security policy interests of the Western alliance. It promoted market economy approaches in developing countries and paid more attention to political loyalty to the Federal Republic than had been the case with the former social-liberal coalition. In terms of content, the discussion went in a different direction. One moved away from the one-sided idea of mainly left-wing politicians that "underdevelopment" had come about solely due to the transmission of Western ideas. Rather, "development also took place in Germany through 'imported' thoughts and political systems—an independent culture arises through exchange and processing, through integration of one's own and foreign, not through demarcation or even the rediscovery of lost paradises" (Heimpel 1983, 5ff).

With the basic guidelines for the Federal Government's development policy of 19 March 1986, the changed conditions were taken into account. The Federal Republic focused on the self-responsibility of the economically "underdeveloped countries", on their own creative forces and the internal framework conditions. The primary goal was to combat economic poverty. However, the affected countries were to help with this task. The Federal Government therefore also relied on non-governmental organisations, which had and have the necessary experience in this "help for self-help". In addition, it increasingly influenced the relevant governments. The primary aim of this aid was food security and rural development, the limitation of population growth and vocational training (BMZ 1991, 11–14).

The 14 November 1961 is considered the birth of the BMZ, when Walter Scheel was appointed the first minister to this office. This also emphasised the growing importance of this sector of German politics externally. However, it took a few more years until the BMZ could actually take the lead in this area, because for the Foreign Office, development policy was an instrument of its foreign policy, especially for the isolation of the GDR in the so-called Third World. Only 3 years after its installation did the BMZ finally receive "overall responsibility for technical assistance, budgetary management of capital aid and for the elaboration of the principles and the programme of development aid" (Buro 1975, 331).

From 1972, the responsibility for the bilateral and multilateral financial cooperation, which had been under the leadership of the Ministry of Economics, was transferred to the Federal Ministry for Economic Cooperation and Development (BMZ). This made the BMZ responsible for the entire planning, the establishment of principles and the coordination of bi- and multilateral development policy. During this period, the Federal Republic of Germany, under the leadership of the BMZ, provided support primarily in two major development policy areas: bilaterally, where about two-thirds of the budget funds were used, and multilaterally, where about one-third of the budget funds were used (BMZ 1991, 19–26).

Bilateral cooperation mainly includes financial cooperation or capital aid in the form of favourable loans, for the economically poorest countries as a grant, for certain projects, programmes and structural aid. In addition, technical cooperation or technical assistance is granted in the form of a grant. This also includes the support of private carriers. Finally, there is also the personal cooperation in the field of training and the deployment of specialists and executives. Multilateral cooperation extends to contributions to international organisations that carry out development projects. These mainly include the United Nations and its specialised agencies (e.g. UNESCO, FAO, ILO, WHO) as well as non-governmental organisations.

The United Nations' target of public development services, making up 0.7% of the gross social product, was never achieved by the Federal Republic of Germany. Although Germany had committed to this goal, in 1990 public development aid was only 0.42% of the gross national product. In comparison, the average for all industrialised countries was 0.35%. However, if one also takes into account private (non-governmental) development contributions, the Federal Republic of Germany achieved a total quota of 0.9% of the gross national product in 1990 (BMZ 1991, 62).

Development Policy of the German Democratic Republic

The Chairman of the GDR Council of Ministers, Willi Stoph, described the GDR's position towards the so-called "Third World" countries as follows: "The GDR is always committed to further strengthening and expanding the alliance with the anti-imperialist states of Asia, Africa and Latin America. We share common goals and interests in the fight against imperialism. Our place is on the side of the states and peoples who are determined to stand up for political and social progress" (Stoph 1972). The two central determinants of GDR foreign policy and thus also the theoretical objectives for economic and social development in the so-called Third World are named here: "anti-imperialist alliances" and "social progress".

The GDR did not use the terms "development aid" and "developing countries" for its development policy in the relevant countries. Instead, it preferred to speak of a special form of "socialist economic aid". The terms developing countries and development aid were for them a form of neo-colonialism and imperialism. From their point of view, development aid from the Western industrial nations was "the state financing of the neo-colonial expansion of imperialism in the interest of monopoly capital and the associated deliveries and services of the imperialist states and international state-monopolistic institutions" (Schütz 1977, 205).

In their opinion, development aid was only a means of imperialism to keep the former colonies in political and economic dependence and to prevent an approach to the socialist states. The release of the former colonies into independence did not, from the GDR's point of view, bring any economic independence for them. Rather, they were mainly kept in dependence under pressure from the "multinational monopolies" in order to maintain their markets and to make a front against the socialist countries (Schütz 1977, 205 f.).

According to the GDR, the developing countries can be divided into four groups:

1. Countries that are moving towards socialism.
2. Countries with capitalist development but "anti-imperialist foreign policy".
3. Countries with an undecided and fluctuating attitude regarding their political path.
4. Countries with a "semi-colonial status" (Ehlert 1979, 243).

For the GDR, "economic aid" was about supporting the developing countries in their "struggle for economic independence from imperialism and economic and social development in contrast to neo-colonialist 'development aid'" (Schütz 1977, p. 1019). In this context, according to the GDR's self-understanding, the support of the state sector and the "imparting [...] of knowledge and experience in the planning and management of the economy" took precedence (Schütz 1977, 1019).

However, their own interests certainly played a not insignificant role, because the GDR was also interested in "long-term economic and trade agreements" as well as in supporting "all democratic and progressive movements against imperialism and for social progress" (Schütz 1977, 1019). The aim was to "win individual developing countries for the 'socialist bloc' in order to weaken the 'basis of imperialism' in the countries of the Third World" and also to "gain access to the raw material markets of the Third World, as well as to sell off favourably those products of the industry of the GDR that were difficult to sell on the ('capitalist') world market" (Federal Ministry for Intra-German Relations 1979, 334).

The GDR's support for so-called developing countries can be seen as antagonistic, as it took place in different areas and there was no unified overarching authority responsible for the implementation. The support for so-called "Third World" countries can be understood as "a mix of solidarity services and commercial relations [...] as well as scientific-technical and cultural measures" (Fröhlich 1993, 150). This view is also held by Claus and Taake, who describe the "cooperation of the GDR" with so-called developing countries as "a broad programme of development aid policy, scientific-technical, commercial, humanitarian and cultural measures" and emphasise that the development policy of the GDR is particularly characterised by its "low coherence" and the "lack of clarity and fragmentation" (1994, 246).

The development policy of the GDR generally first included loans, which "[...] are granted within the framework of agreements on economic and scientific-technical cooperation [...]" (Bellers 1988, 31–33). These were mostly granted in the form of "goods and supply credits" and were linked to services from the GDR. Another element was the "Brigades of Friendship" of the FDJ (Free German Youth), which can be compared in the broadest sense with the "development workers" in the Western understanding. They participated in the implementation of the support for so-called developing countries, especially in the construction of infrastructural projects. In the event of natural disasters, the GDR also provided direct aid, i.e. disaster relief such as cash donations ("Solidarpfennig"), food or medicine deliveries (Obernhummer 2010, 7).

Until the mid-1950s, the countries of the so-called Third World played virtually no role for the GDR in terms of development policy. On the one hand, the GDR was economically weakened by the consequences of the Second World War and the subsequent dismantling and reparations to the Soviet Union to such an extent that it did not have the appropriate basis for aid. Essentially as a reaction to the "Truman Doctrine" of the USA, which called for a global containment of communism, the "Two Camp Theory" was proclaimed in 1947 on the occasion of the founding conference of the "Communist Information Bureau" (Cominform). According to this, the world was divided into a capitalist and a socialist camp. The new independent states were also classified under this aspect (Spanger and Brock 1987, 160 f.).

Only with the Bandung conference in 1955 and the Colombo conference in 1962 did it become clear to the Eastern Bloc—and thus also to the GDR—that a new, a third, force was beginning to emerge in the international power concert. Since this point, the GDR tried to establish and expand its relations with the states of the so-called Third World. However, the Federal Republic's claim to sole representation with the "Hallstein Doctrine" posed a significant obstacle at the international level. Therefore, it tried to play the "anti-imperialist" card and support the peoples in their national liberation struggle. After all, it managed to conclude some long-term trade and payment agreements in the mid-1950s (Spanger and Brock 1987, 163).

The 1960s are characterised by the effort to break through the Hallstein Doctrine. To this end, the GDR developed a lively travel diplomacy to various countries of the so-called Third World. Here, the travels of Margarete Wittkowski (formerly Deputy Chairwoman of the Council of Ministers, then President of the State Bank of the GDR) in 1964, 1966 and 1967 to India, Sri Lanka (formerly Ceylon), Myanmar (formerly Burma) and Cambodia are to be mentioned. In addition, other officials and diplomats travelled to these countries as well as to Indonesia (Max Sefrin, Peter Florin). In 1968, Foreign Minister Winzer travelled to Burma, Cambodia and India. India in particular was courted by the GDR, resulting in state trade agreements and training aid. However, these were rather modest compared to the aid from the Federal Republic amounting to 4 billion DM by 1968 (Ludwig 1968, 311ff.).

The Arab Near East enjoyed special attention. The outstanding event of the travel activity was the visit of the Chairman of the State Council Walter Ulbricht to Egypt in February 1965 to the Egyptian President Nasser. Despite the state guest being received with all protocolary honours, Egypt did not recognise the GDR under international law, even after Egypt's break with Bonn a year later. But the state visit brought about a yearly growing trade exchange and the training of Egyptian technicians of various disciplines.

Although Foreign Minister Winzer spent several weeks in Egypt and Syria at the beginning of 1969, full diplomatic recognition was not forthcoming. Nevertheless, GDR-Egypt trade alone grew by 25% from 1968 to 1969 to 350 million Valuta-Mark (Reinhardt 1969, 330 f.). The GDR tried to present itself as a natural ally of the decolonised states. The Chairman of the State Council Walter Ulbricht stated on 26 September 1960 before the Diplomatic Corps of the GDR:

The German Democratic Republic follows a different tradition of the German people in relation to the countries and peoples who are languishing under colonial oppression and are leading their national liberation struggle, namely the tradition of the German working class, the German humanists, who always despised and fought against colonial oppression and exploitation, who always championed the sacred right of the colonially oppressed peoples to freedom, human dignity, and a nationally independent happy life of all peoples. Based on this good humanistic German tradition, the German Democratic Republic promotes to the best of its ability everywhere and at all times the young nation-states and the peoples fighting for freedom and justice (Spanger and Brock 1987, 165)

Overall, the GDR was able to establish itself as a partner on a modest scale in the Arab states of Egypt and Syria as well as the South and East Asian countries of India, Sri Lanka (formerly Ceylon), Myanmar (formerly Burma), Cambodia and Indonesia in the 1960s. All these states pursued a form of moderate state socialism or a sharp anti-Western policy due to foreign policy differences with their former colonial powers, the USA or Israel. By the late 1960s, the GDR still had not succeeded in securing its key objective of international legal recognition, despite its efforts.

Through the détente policy in the first half of the 1970s and the conclusion of the Basic Treaty between the Federal Republic and the GDR in 1972, the latter was upgraded internationally. Most countries in the world established official diplomatic relations with the GDR. It was also recognised in the GDR that worldwide peace could only be maintained if the various problems of the Third World were solved. In the GDR, it was acknowledged that global peace could only be preserved by resolving the challenges faced by the Third World. Nonetheless, as Spanger and Brock (1987, 168) point out, this consensus did not conceal the significant differences in how the East and West assessed the means and strategies to achieve this.

The GDR did indeed demand the expansion of détente worldwide and to use the experiences gathered on the European continent, but it opposed development policy cooperation with the West following the European model. The prerequisite for détente and development in the so-called Third World from the perspective of the GDR represents "the elimination of the remnants of 'classical' colonial and racist foreign rule and the pushing back of neocolonialism" (Dreifahl and Schilling 1976, 663).

The path to this goal was thus embedded in the path of Marxism-Leninism. The GDR used its new international reputation for intensive engagement within the division of labour of the Warsaw Pact states, especially in the African states that turned to the socialist camp. These were Ethiopia, Angola and Mozambique (Belal 1981).

The support that the GDR had provided for the liberation movements in these states now paid off after the overthrow of Emperor Haile Selassie in Ethiopia and the withdrawal of the Portuguese from Angola and Mozambique. Only in the policy before the independence of Zimbabwe had the GDR miscalculated. Hoping for access to the country's rich mineral resources, it had backed the wrong horse in the liberation struggle. Instead of Nkomo's ZAPU, which the GDR had exclusively supported, Mugabe's ZANU prevailed. Despite the rapid diplomatic recognition of independent Zimbabwe and also the commitment in favour of the ANC in South

Africa, the GDR failed to achieve a similar position in this part of southern Africa as in the other three mentioned countries (Post and Sandvoss 1982, 24–26; Spanger and Brock 1987, 171).

The policy of the GDR in Africa was not spared setbacks. Thus, the sometimes obvious interference in the internal affairs of some African states such as the DR Congo (formerly Zaire) or disappointed development policy expectations as in the case of the Central African Republic led to the breaking off of diplomatic relations by these states. Similar conflicts existed with Ghana as early as 1966, as well as with Zambia in 1971 and Morocco in 1975. The direct interference of the Soviet Union in conjunction with its allies on the African continent also raised fears of a "red belt" and an "axis Moscow-Havana-East Berlin".

While the GDR pursued the path of détente in Europe and presented itself as a cooperative partner in the intra-German treaties and its entry into the United Nations and the CSCE (Conference on Security and Co-operation in Europe), it relied on "anti-imperialist optimism" in Southeast Asia (Vietnam, Laos, Cambodia) and Africa (Löwis of Menar 1977, 647.). Erich Honecker saw "strategic defeats of imperialism in Africa and Indochina". Especially Africa, "whose peoples make a significant contribution to the progress of humanity and to the further change of the international balance of power", was seen as a "centre of great class struggles", in which socialism increasingly found better fighting conditions (Spanger and Brock 1987, 171).

Although the GDR achieved some successes in 'anti-imperialist' states, its commitment to development policy was limited, largely due to its economic structure and integration into the Eastern economic system. Hillebrand (1987, 130) notes that this integration negatively impacted the GDR's international competitiveness by restricting access to Western technology, which was essential for scientific and technical advancement.

The 1970s included for the GDR both in Europe and in the so-called Third World overall the breakthrough at diplomatic and partly also economic level. In contrast, the 1980s are marked by severe setbacks. A significant milestone in the GDR's approach to the so-called Third World was Erich Honecker's trips to Ethiopia and South Yemen at the end of 1979, when the Chairman of the State Council inaugurated the first Karl Marx monument on the African continent in Addis Ababa, in the presence of head of state Mengistu. The official guest from socialist Germany was able to reflect on 'the growth and prosperity of the socialist world system' on the African continent (Löwis of Menar 1980, 42).

A severe setback for the entire socialist camp, both in the West and especially in the so-called Third World, was the invasion of the Soviet Union at the turn of the year 1979/1980 in Afghanistan. Already at the fifth World Trade Conference in 1979 in Manila, numerous "Third World" countries distanced themselves from the socialist countries due to their inadequate development policy commitments. The initial euphoria of the 1970s had faded when numerous developing countries noticed that the achievements of the socialist states fell far short of expectations. "From a development policy perspective, however, the intervention rather indicated a not untypical weakness of the socialist states in the Third World, as they failed to effectively influence the development of Afghanistan with means other than military ones. Similar experiences had to be made by the socialist states in southern Africa" (Spanger 1984, 47).

The restrictive energy policy of the Soviet Union at the beginning of the 1980s towards the GDR, reducing oil deliveries by 10% compared to the original volume agreed for 1983, the failure of Polish deliveries of raw materials and semifinished goods and the massive reduction of Western material imports due to the shortage of foreign exchange, led to significant supply shortages in the GDR (Buck 1983, 53). From this point of view, the Middle East trip of the Chairman of the State Council Honecker in October 1982 to Syria, Cyprus and Kuwait should also be considered. However, the (foreign) economic success of this visit was moderate (Ammer 1982, 1319 f.).

The GDR maintained significant cooperation with a total of 30 states of the so-called Third World, with seven of them having particularly intensive relations. These countries were Ethiopia, Angola, Mozambique, Nicaragua, Cuba, Mongolia and Vietnam. The cooperation extended over a broad programme, which included both development policy and scientific-technical, trade policy and cultural measures.

A central aspect of this cooperation was the training of students from these countries at the technical and higher education institutions of the GDR. This training served not only for professional qualification but also for the promotion of long-term relationships and the ideology of the GDR. By attending technical and higher education institutions, the students from the Third World countries gained access to specific knowledge and technological know-how, which they could use in their home countries (Lange 1985).

The development policy cooperation also included the exchange of experts, support in the construction of infrastructure projects and technical assistance and advice in various areas such as agriculture, health care and education. In addition, trade relations were promoted, with the GDR exporting products and technologies to the affected countries and enabling imports of raw materials and other goods.

At the cultural level, artistic and cultural exchange programmes took place, which contributed to deepening the understanding and relationships between the participating countries. This intensive cooperation was not only a political strategy of the GDR but also a means of supporting and strengthening the partner countries in the global context of the Cold War (Claus and Taake 1993, 246).

In the 1980s, the GDR adapted its strategy towards the countries of the so-called Third World, after it had become apparent that these countries were not tending towards socialism as quickly as hoped, especially in Africa, where such developments seemed likely in the 1970s. The GDR now focused more on securing sources of raw materials and finding markets for its own products, without having to rely on foreign exchange.

As part of this approach, the GDR offered its partner countries capital goods and technical know-how. Through the exchange of capital goods and knowledge, the GDR was able to strengthen its own interests by gaining access to important raw materials and simultaneously creating markets for its own products. This model was aimed at strengthening the economic interests of the GDR and improving its position in international trade (Kant 1979).

For the partner countries, this cooperation also brought benefits with it. They gained access to technologies and capital goods, which helped them to increase their productivity and economic development. In addition, they were able to place their own products on the GDR market and thus gained access to an alternative sales market.

From the GDR's point of view, this type of cooperation also contributed to the stabilisation of the socialist bloc. Through the establishment of economic relations and the mutual exchange of goods and services, the bond between the socialist countries was strengthened. This model enabled the GDR to consolidate its position in the international context and at the same time to contribute to the support of other socialist countries.

Overall, this new orientation of GDR policy in the 1980s was characterised by a pragmatic economic approach, which aimed to improve the economic strength of the GDR and at the same time to strengthen relations with the countries of the so-called Third World (Claus and Taake 1993, 255).

Similarities and Differences in the Development Policy of the Two German States

The development policy in the Federal Republic of Germany was and is characterised by the diversity and plurality of its liberal society. In contrast to a uniform, consistent concept of state development policy, a variety of other groups and institutions are involved in this area, including transnational corporations, churches, trade unions, political parties and foundations. These actors each bring different perspectives, goals and approaches to development cooperation, leading to a multilayered and dynamic landscape.

In the GDR, development policy was strongly embedded in the ideology and goals of the socialist bloc, as the country was socially, politically and economically led by a relatively homogeneous group that represented the principles of Marxism-Leninism. In contrast to the Federal Republic, the GDR did not have a separate ministry that dealt exclusively with development policy.

The development policy of the GDR was rather coordinated by the Ministry for Foreign Affairs (MfAA), which was responsible for the overall foreign policy. Within the MfAA, there were departments or units that dealt with specific aspects of international cooperation and development. These departments worked closely with other ministries and institutions to implement the development policy goals of the GDR (Lange 1985).

The GDR pursued an ideologically motivated development policy, which aimed to strengthen solidarity and cooperation between the socialist countries and to promote the influence of socialism in the world. This was reflected in the development policy measures, which focused on the exchange of experts, education and cultural programmes as well as economic cooperation (Claus and Taake 1993, 253ff).

A central element of GDR development policy was the support of "brother countries", especially in Africa, Latin America and Asia. The GDR offered technical assistance, training programmes and financial support for infrastructure projects in these countries. This often happened within the framework of bilateral agreements or multilateral cooperation within the socialist bloc.

The development policy of the GDR was strongly influenced by the ideology of socialism and stood in contrast to the capitalist development policy of the Federal Republic. It was seen as a means to promote the worldwide spread of socialism and to strengthen international solidarity among socialist countries. The close connection between foreign policy and development aid was a characteristic feature of GDR policy and reflected the unified leadership and ideology of the country.

Instead, the goals were formulated by the SED (Socialist Unity Party of Germany), and various ministries were entrusted with the practical implementation. Societal organisations also played a role in this field, being closely intertwined with the state structures and political objectives. These contrasting developments illustrate the different political, societal and ideological framework conditions under which development policy in both German states was shaped during the Cold War.

During the détente phase of the 1970s, both German states agreed to avoid confrontation in the so-called developing countries and to strive for a lasting cooperation of the North and the South. An agreement on the way there was omitted, as both sides did not want to give up their actual objectives, which resulted from their societal system. Common to the Federal Republic and the GDR was the increasingly intensive scientific engagement with the issues of developing countries. The increasing critical distance of the developing countries to the socialist states at the end of the 1970s, beginning of the 1980s, with the demand for stronger economic support and abstention from direct interference in their internal affairs strengthened the West German position in development policy.

The new guidelines for the development policy of the FRG from 1986, and also after reunification, focus on the promotion of their own creative forces and the responsibility of the developing countries: "Help for self-help". All federal governments have repeatedly emphasised the independent path of the developing countries and their right to self-determination (Spanger and Brock 1987, 332).

For the GDR, development aid was ultimately a tool for promoting its ideological and political struggle. The GDR pursued specific transformation ideas, which were based on the central importance of internal political factors for securing power. Party relations were used to provide material, personnel and ideological support in the emergence of Marxist-Leninist vanguard parties. From this perspective, the development aid of the GDR followed its state-centric ideas (Spanger 1984, 152).

The ideological differences in understanding the respective development ideas between the FRG's "development (aid) policy" and the GDR's communist−/socialist-influenced "solidarity" concepts can finally be illustrated by an article from the Johannesburg Sunday Times, dated 21 September 1975. The article titled "White Bushman King exiled" describes the story of Hans-Joachim Heinz, a

German parasitologist, who for over 15 years stood for his very own development (aid) policy with the!Ko, an ethnic group in the Central Kalahari (Botswana). Heinz caused the!Ko—who had a nomadic economy—to settle down, encouraged the!Ko to produce arrows and bows for sale to tourists and married Namkwa, the daughter of a!Ko chief (Büschel 2008, 333).

The Botswana government expelled Heinz in 1975 from Brere and thus also from the settlement of the!Ko he had founded. Liz Wiley, a development worker from New Zealand appointed by the Botswana government, had demanded the immediate expulsion of the "German Bushman King". He would have—despite all good intentions—ignored the peculiarity of the!Ko and their concept of collective property, maintained an authoritarian leadership style and shown outright colonial chauvinism and sexism. Arrogantly and obstinately, he would have promoted the destruction of the indigenous culture. He alone was responsible for the "Tragedy of the Bushmen", the "loss" of their traditional culture, their disorientation and their alcoholism (Sporton et al. 1999, 441–459). Heinz himself later admitted that he had not been "uninvolved" in this "Tragedy of the Bushmen" (Heinz and Lee 1984, 303).

The then director of the Max Planck Institute for Behavioural Physiology, Irenäus Eibl-Eibesfeldt, to whom Heinz had provided contacts with the!Ko, had a different view and regretted emphatically that the government of Botswana had relied on the opinion and demand of a "communist ideologue" like Liz Wiley. After the end of Heinz's "development project", the!Ko had "fallen back" into their hunter-gatherer existence. They lived "but no longer with the carefreeness and satisfaction of the past" but were "aimless" and "depressed", because the "few years of development" had "alienated them from their old life". According to Eibl-Eibesfeldt, a few more years of Heinz's "friendly authoritarian leadership" would have been necessary to put the!Ko on a sustainable path of economic development. Because unlike the communist Wiley, who would have wanted to realise her ideas of collective property, Heinz knew about the "pronounced individuality of the bush people" and recognised that only "through the incentive of individual ownership were successes to be achieved" (Heinz and Lee 1984, 9).

In summary, it should be emphasised that the training of those individuals who, in the 1960s and 1970s, were active in development policy—both from the FRG and the GDR—before their deployment in development projects, was in direct continuity with colonialism and sometimes also with National Socialism. The training included regional studies, writings on tropical hygiene, behavioural instructions in dealing with Africans and discussions about cultural differences and their alleged inhibitory effect on development, with these contents fluctuating between more or less clear physical, psychological, cultural and social racisms. Even under the guise of cooperation, the supposed superiority of one's own "essence" and one's own path of development was emphasised (Büschel 2008, 364 f.).

These ideas of progress and development led to structures being created in the efforts to implement them practically, which excluded and devalued certain groups. Both the actors from the FRG and the GDR ultimately held on to their belief in the effectiveness and beneficence of development policy measures. Despite all (self-)

criticism and concerns, a commitment to concrete aids such as artificial fertilisers, combine harvesters, X-ray machines or slide rules was often evident.

The ideas of progress and development were often shaped by a Western-influenced modernisation thinking, which often went hand in hand with a sense of superiority. This mindset was reflected in the idea that Western technologies and methods were the key to economic development and prosperity in developing countries. However, this led to structures and actions that portrayed certain groups or cultures as backward or less developed and contributed to their exclusion.

Both in the FRG and in the GDR, development policy measures were often seen as altruistic help and contribution to global progress. Despite the criticism of the underlying ideologies and power structures of development aid, the belief in the usefulness and effect of these measures remained. The emphasis on concrete aids such as artificial fertilisers, combine harvesters, X-ray machines or slide rules in development cooperation reflected the technologically oriented view of progress and development. These objects were often seen as symbols of modern life and industrial civilisation and were intended to benefit developing countries to increase their productivity and improve living conditions (Gieler 2023, 35–42).

Overall, these considerations show how the concepts of development and willingness to help were often shaped by a certain technological and modernisation-focused thinking, which was, however, simultaneously accompanied by structures of exclusion and devaluation. The enduring belief in the effectiveness of development policy measures reflected the conviction that technological progress and material support were the keys to development and improving living conditions in the so-called developing countries (Büschel 2008, 365).

References

Ammer, T. (1982). Die Nahost-Reise Honeckers im Oktober 1982. Deutschland Archiv. Zeitschrift für Fragen der DDR und der Deutschlandpolitik, 12, 1313ff.
Belal, A. R. A. (1981). Zur Analyse des Verhältnisses sozialistischer Länder – Entwicklungsländer am Beispiel der Herausbildung und Entwicklung der Entwicklungsländerwissenschaften der Deutschen Demokratischen Republik (1945–1974). Frankfurt.
Bellers, J. (Hrsg.). (1988). Entwicklungshilfe – Politik in Europa. Studien zur Politikwissenschaft Bd. 21. Münster.
Bodemer, K. (1974). Entwicklungshilfe – Politik für wen? Ideologie und Vergabepraxis der deutschen Entwicklungshilfe in der ersten Dekade. München.
Buck, H. (1983). Abbau von Rohstoffengpässen durch Handel mit Entwicklungsländern, DDR-Wirtschaftsbeziehungen mit Entwicklungsländern am Beispiel Syriens, Zyperns und Kuweits. Deutschland Archiv. Zeitschrift für Fragen der DDR und der Deutschlandpolitik, 1, 53ff.
Bundesministerium für wirtschaftliche Zusammenarbeit. (1991). Journalisten-Handbuch Entwicklungspolitik 1991/92. Informationen über die Dritte Welt. Bonn.
Buro, A. (1975). Die Entwicklungspolitik der Bundesrepublik Deutschland. In B. Tibi & V. Brandes (Hrsg.), Politische Ökonomie. Geschichte und Kritik. Handbuch 2 – Unterentwicklung (328–348). Frankfurt.
Büschel, H. (2008). In Afrika helfen. Akteure westdeutscher „Entwicklungshilfe" und ostdeutscher „Solidarität" 1955–1975. Archiv für Sozialgeschichte, 48, 333–365.

Claus, B., & Taake, H.-H. (1993). Die Entwicklungspolitik der DDR – Ein Rückblick. In U. van der Heyden, I. Schleicher, & H.-G. Schleicher (Hrsg.), Die DDR und Afrika. Zwischen Klassenkampf und neuem Denken (122–153). Münster.

Ehlert, W. (1979). Wörterbuch der Ökonomie. Sozialismus*(4th ed.). Berlin (Ost).

Eppler, E. (1971). Wenig Zeit für die Dritte Welt. Stuttgart.

Fröhlich, B. (1993). Gedanken zur Entwicklungszusammenarbeit der DDR mit Afrika. In U. van der Heyden, I., & H.-G. Schleicher (Hrsg.), Die DDR und Afrika. Zwischen Klassenkampf und neuem Denken (188–202). Hamburg.

Galbraith, J. K. (1980). Die Arroganz der Satten. München.

Gieler, W. (2010). Entwicklungspolitik der Bundesrepublik Deutschland. Die Bedeutung der 25 Thesen von Gymnich für den Wandel in der deutschen Entwicklungspolitik. Bonn.

Gieler, W. (2023). Reguliertes Chaos: (Re-)Konstruktionen zum westlichen Ethnozentrismus (2nd ed.). Bonn.

Heimpel, C. (1983). Deutsche Entwicklungshilfe vor der Wende? Aus Politik und Zeitgeschichte, B 23.

Heinz, H. J., & Lee, M. (1984). Namkwa. Ein Leben unter Buschmännern. München.

Hillebrand, E. (1987). Das Afrika-Engagement der DDR. Frankfurt.

Kant, H. (1979). Die Wirtschaftspolitik der DDR in den siebziger Jahren. Berlin.

Lange, M. (1985). Planung und Außenhandel in der DDR: Eine Studie zur Bedeutung der Planung im System des internationalen Handels der DDR. Berlin.

Löwis of Menar, H. v. (1977). Solidarität und Subversion. Die Rolle der DDR im südlichen Afrika. Deutschland Archiv. Zeitschrift für Fragen der DDR und der Deutschlandpolitik, 6, 643ff.

Löwis of Menar, H. v. (1980). Die DDR als Schrittmacher im weltrevolutionären Prozeß. Zur Honecker-Visite in Äthiopien und im Südjemen. Deutschland Archiv. Zeitschrift für Fragen der DDR und der Deutschlandpolitik, 1, 40ff.

Ludwig, H. (1968). Beziehungen zu Entwicklungsländern. Die DDR in Asien. Deutschland Archiv. Zeitschrift für Fragen der DDR und der Deutschlandpolitik, 3, 310ff.

Obernhummer, I. C. (2010). Experten der „wissenschaftlich-technischen Zusammenarbeit" der DDR in Afrika. Alltag und Lebensweisen zwischen DDR-Richtlinien und angespannter Sicherheitslage in den 1970er und 1980er Jahren. Wien.

Otto, J. (2018). Fortbildungen als Entwicklungshilfe – Fachkräfte aus Afrika, Asien und Lateinamerika in der Bundesrepublik und der DDR. Deutschland Archiv. Zeitschrift für Fragen der DDR und der Deutschlandpolitik.

Post, U., & Sandvoss, F. (1982). Die Afrikapolitik der DDR. Hamburg.

Reinhardt, H. (1969). Winzers Mission im Nahen Osten. Deutschland Archiv. Zeitschrift für Fragen der DDR und der Deutschlandpolitik, 3, 330ff.

Richter, M. (2019). Die Entwicklungspolitik der DDR im Kontext des Kalten Krieges: Eine Analyse der ideologischen und geopolitischen Dimensionen. Zeitschrift für Ostforschung, 68 (2), 245–263.

Schütz, G. (Hrsg.). (1977). Kleines Politisches Wörterbuch (3rd ed.). Berlin (Ost).

Simon, K. (1981). Entwicklungspolitische Strategien von Regierung und Parteien in der Bundesrepublik Deutschland. Aus Politik und Zeitgeschichte, 34.

Sohn, K.-H. (1973). Theorie und Praxis der deutschen Entwicklungshilfe (2nd ed). München.

Spanger, H.-J. (1984). Die beiden Deutschen Staaten in der Dritten Welt. Deutschland Archiv. Zeitschrift für Fragen der DDR und der Deutschlandpolitik, 1, 30–50.

Spanger, H.-J., & Brock, L. (1987). Die beiden deutschen Staaten in der Dritten Welt. Die Entwicklungspolitik der DDR — eine Herausforderung für die Bundesrepublik Deutschland? Opladen.

Sporton, D. S., Thomas, D., & Morrison, J. (1999). Outcomes of Social and Environmental Change in the Kalahari of Botswana. The Role of Migration. Journal of Southern African Studies, 25, 441–459.

Stoph, W. (1972). Mit guter Bilanz voran auf dem klaren Kurs des VIII. Parteitages. Neues Deutschland.

Chapter 4
Development Policy in Reunified Germany Between 1990 and 2021

Meik Nowak

Abstract The focus is on the analysis of the first 31 years of German state development policy after the end of the East-West confrontation and the reunification of Germany. From a contemporary historical perspective, global political changes and the transformation processes of the ministerial self-understanding are evaluated. In addition, key interfaces to other policy areas, such as security policy after 11 September 2001, and the global role of binding development goals such as the MDGs up to the SDGs and the global changes caused by the COVID-19 pandemic are in focus.

Contemporary Historical Classification

This contemporary historical outline of German state development cooperation includes not only the four different ministers with diverging political viewpoints and personal emphases of the respective development policy concepts but also a multitude of external political as well as economic and societal events of global significance. This chapter is to be understood as an institutionalised and contemporary historical overview. The 31 years between the end of the Cold War in 1990 and the end of Minister Müller's tenure in 2021 with the transition to the traffic light coalition can be divided into at least three phases.

These phases are roughly outlined as follows:

1. Phase "Development Cooperation as Global Regulatory Policy"
2. Phase "Development Cooperation as Preventive Security Policy"
3. Phase "Development Cooperation as Global Sustainability Policy"

M. Nowak (✉)
Geistes- und Sozialwissenschaften, Helmut-Schmidt-Universität, Hamburg, Hamburg, Germany
e-mail: nowakme@hsu-hh.de

On a national level, this period covers the Spranger era in the last two cabinets of Helmut Kohl, a time marked by the German reunification with the merging of formerly West Germany (FRG) and East Germany (GDR) into a reunified, united Germany. This domestic and societal challenge of reunification also had its influence on the importance and design of German state development cooperation (Bücking 1998).

In foreign policy, this first decade is marked by a significant increase in international conferences on global issues and economic globalisation, the much-invoked end of history (Fukuyama 1992) and a flare-up of many wars in countries of the Global South. Even within Europe, crises and wars marked the last decade of the last century. The former Yugoslav state territory broke apart. In 1991, the 10-day war in Slovenia took place, from 1991 to 1995 the Croatian War, from 1992 to 1995 the Bosnian War and from 1992 to 1994 the Croatian-Bosniak War within the Bosnian War. Finally, from 1998 to 1999 the Kosovo War took place with the military Operation Allied Force (OAF) of NATO against the then Federal Republic of Yugoslavia.

The 1990s of German state development cooperation can therefore be summarised both under Minister Spranger and then the subsequent red-green federal government and the takeover of the BMZ's business by Minister Wieczorek-Zeul from 1998 as development from the predicted end of history (Fukuyama 1992) towards a more purposeful German development policy. This goes hand in hand with the special role of the many international (world) conferences in the context of the United Nations in the 1990s.

These include the Conference on Environment and Development in Rio de Janeiro (1992), the Vienna Human Rights Conference (1993), the Conference on Population and Development in Cairo (1994), the Conference on Social Development in Copenhagen (1995), the World Women's Conference in Beijing (1995), the UN Conference on Human Settlements in Istanbul "HABITAT" (1996) and the World Food Conference in Rome (1996). Many international insights and solutions at these conferences were in line with the development policy criteria and priorities of the BMZ in relation to multilateral politics—this is certainly a merit of Minister Spranger.

This attribution of a targeted and focused German development policy at the end of the 1990s falls into the era of Heidemarie Wieczorek-Zeul, in which development policy was understood as global structural policy or world domestic policy. In 2000, the MDGs gradually became the guiding principle for the design of the state development policy programmes of Germany and other OECD donors.

Reinold E. Thiel accurately analyses this time, especially the intense discussion about existing and alternative development concepts at national and international level. This is also a critique of traditional development concepts, the reception of the Human Development Index as a new methodological framework and the path to the MDGs as a new and above all binding and targeted development strategy.

> In German development policy, which has realigned its goals after the change of government in 1998, there are certainly similarities to the new strategic approaches of the World Bank and DAC. The policy of Minister Heidemarie Wieczorek-Zeul and State Secretary

Uschi Eid is, with their strong emphasis on poverty reduction, crisis prevention, debt relief and civil society participation, certainly people-oriented. What they have lacked so far is a well-thought-out coherent concept, as the World Bank has now presented. This cannot be designed overnight, and certainly the ministry should be granted the necessary time for this. But this requires not only time, but also minds. (Thiel 2001, 32)

Of further great development policy significance is at strategic level the overcoming of the "Washington Consensus" and the purely economic view of development. This hopeful discussion about debt relief, new development models and people-centred development was overshadowed by the geopolitical reality of 11 September 2001 and the resulting focus on development policy as peace policy in the context of security policy. The design and implementation of the MDGs was certainly, alongside the reconstruction of a democratic Afghan state, the dominant theme of the years 2001 to 2009 (Bohnet 2015). Following on from this, there was a sharp turn in German development cooperation after 2009. The following quote from the Heidelberg speech of the then Minister Niebel summarises the differences very succinctly and also explains the reluctance of many development policy actors with the FDP-led ministry between 2009 and 2013:

I don't like the word development "aid". It divides the world into helpers and those in need of help. Against such thinking, one of the famous Heidelberg economists aptly objected: "If you need a helping hand—look for it first at the end of your right arm!" In the development cooperation of the past, the help-seeking right or left hands were trusted too much to hold out their hands and too little to take action. But we cannot develop a country from the outside. We can provide support for self-help. I interpret the Z in the name of the BMZ as it was originally intended: economic cooperation, not repeated additional payment. The direction is: Away from the supervised social case, towards the active citizen. (Niebel 2011)

The Niebel era after the election victory of the black-yellow coalition in the 2009 federal election was seen by many actors in development cooperation as a polarising and also misunderstood time. The following quote embodies a part of this time very clearly:

The daily newspapers emphasised in their evaluation both the attempted carpet smuggling of the Minister as well as the structural reforms leading to the establishment of the Society for International Cooperation (GIZ). Beyond scandalised individual aspects in the management of the Ministry by the FDP politician Dirk Niebel […]. (Brämer and Ziai 2015, 400).

Whether these 4 years are just an exception in the relationship between nongovernmental and governmental actors of German development cooperation, or whether structural features of the former minister's work beyond the creation of the GIZ are still held in the ministry 7 years later, is certainly debatable. The time after 2013 and the renewed grand coalition brought Gerd Müller into office as the responsible minister. From the beginning of his term, he focused—unlike his predecessors Niebel and Wieczorek-Zeul—on sustainability issues and, as the first politician of the first rank after former Federal President Horst Köhler (2004–2010), put Africa in the regional focus of German development and foreign policy. His first years were marked by the implementation and evaluation of the MDGs, the intensive technical discussion about the conception of the SDGs as a successor concept of globally binding guidelines and the increasingly strong discussion of climate change, climate adaptation and climate policy in the context of development policy beyond environmental and economic policy.

The 1990s: Global Regulatory Policy

Referring to the time after 1990, Fukuyama has argued that the future history of mankind will be characterised by a victory march of economic and political liberalism, which will now spread worldwide after the end of communism. When the Western version of democracy has established itself as a form of government everywhere, the final form of human society (Fukuyama 1992) has been reached. This would then be the end of history. Since the revolutions of the Enlightenment—and here especially the French Revolution—only two principles have guided historical development. This is, on the one hand, a scientific way of thinking, which leads to permanent technological progress and—as a result—to the desire for general education.

The other principle is the individual's striving for recognition, which then socially aims at the emergence of constitutional democracies and the protection of individual personality and freedom rights. As a natural law, political liberalisation follows economic liberalism, which must exist as a basic condition for political and social freedom (Fukuyama 1992). As empirical evidence of this development—which still holds today in political discussion—the countries of Southeast Asia were mentioned. There, the "common marketisation" has brought about the formation of modern democracies, something that was also expected from the Soviet Union and China based on the reforms of Gorbachev and Deng Xiaoping.

Building on this, the integration of the development policy content and programmes of the former GDR into overall German development cooperation was seen more as a symbolic problem for the actors of development cooperation but certainly a real problem in the focus countries of the so-called socialist brotherly aid. The former GDR had a significant cooperation with a total of 30 Third World countries, concerning trade and exchange of specialists and executives as well as military aid. But only with seven countries was it intensive and noteworthy structured.

These were mainly since the end of the 1970s Ethiopia, Angola, Mozambique, Nicaragua, Cuba, Mongolia and the Socialist Republic of Vietnam (Bücking 1998). Since the development aid of the former GDR was not centrally organised through a ministry but decentralised through individual specialist areas in the relevant national departments, the institutional anchoring was different and—at least for the absorption of the former East German development cooperation—very strongly country-oriented. The development policy measures were usually broadly based programmes, in which both development policy and scientific-technical, trade policy and cultural individual measures were bundled and politically justified (Bohnet 2015).

A large number of development-relevant measures was taken up alongside the classic labour migration of contract workers, the mostly polytechnic education at the technical and higher education institutions of the former GDR. After reunification, development cooperation with these seven countries was therefore reduced from the perspective of the partner countries, which were then still called recipient countries, and restructured by Germany. This included sometimes massive cuts in the funding volumes and significantly influenced German state development cooperation with these countries in the 1990s (Bohnet 2015). With the disintegration of the former Soviet Union and the political-social transformation of the former states of the Eastern Bloc in Central and Eastern Europe but also in Central Asia, new partner countries of German development cooperation emerged, in which knowledge of planned economic processes and mastery of the Russian language were a defining characteristic (Bücking 1998).

In terms of content, the focus on poverty reduction was dominant in the 1990s—accompanied by the discussion about the importance of environmental and climate issues as well as the question of the role of the United Nations and peacekeeping within the framework of development policy. The policy fields "climate and environment", "peace and security" and "democracy and human rights" became increasingly cross-cutting parts of the German development discourse, which was reflected between new multilateral possibilities and classic bilateral traditions—especially in technical and personnel cooperation—in German development cooperation.

In foreign policy, the dissolution of the Soviet Union with the accompanying detachment of the former constituent states from the USSR in Central Asia and the Caucasus was a dominant factor, which dissolved socialist or Marxist-Leninist political designs in many African and Arab countries and included a new wave of democratisation and liberalisation in these very countries (Woyke 2016). Together with the first development report and the creation of the Human Development Index, 1990 was a remarkable year in which a new concept in the sense of world governance was created, starting with the World Children's Summit in New York as the start of the world conferences of the 1990s. The Washington Consensus of the International Monetary Fund, the World Bank and American government institutions on neoliberalism heralded—albeit under different auspices—a different development policy, indeed a creation of a new geopolitical environment. But as early as 1992, the concept of sustainable development adopted at the second UN Conference on Environment and Development in Rio de Janeiro was formed, and the Local Agenda 21 was the declaration of intent for the twenty-first century on the immediate relevance of climate protection, biodiversity and forest protection. The Rio Summit—also Earth Summit—marks the peak of a worldwide interest in world conferences as policy-formulating institutions (Stockmann et al. 2016; Woyke 2016).

In 1992, the then UN Secretary-General Boutros-Ghali published the "Agenda for Peace", which was created at the suggestion of the then US President Bush (sen.). The core messages of this agenda were the demand for preventive diplomacy and the goal of creating peace, maintaining peace and building peace in the phase after a conflict. However, the failure of the UN intervention in Somalia led to scepticism about the success of humanitarian interventions and clearly showed a gap between civilian and military approaches to ending warlike conflicts (Stockmann et al. 2016).

In addition, the question of challenges of development policy in fragile states or the role of development policy organisations in warlike conflicts was raised for the first time—which later resulted in the role of development cooperation organisations in Rwanda in 1994 and the resulting approach of "do no harm" as a guiding principle for actors of development cooperation and humanitarian aid resonated like a thunderclap (Woyke 2016).

However, before that, 1993 was recognised as an important historical moment when apartheid in South Africa ended and the protection of human rights was discussed as a goal of development cooperation at the UN Conference on Human Rights in Vienna. This led to the discussion about the protection and also violation of human rights becoming a new field in development policy and led to an increased political conditioning of development cooperation. On 23 January 1993, the BMZ also received its full name to this day, "Federal Ministry for Economic Cooperation and Development" (Bohnet 2015). The following years were then characterised—based on the impression of the genocide in Rwanda and the ethnic cleansing in the post-Yugoslav wars—by a stronger interlinking of development, peace and security policy with humanitarian aid (Stockmann et al. 2016).

End of the 1990s and Beginning of the Noughties: Global Structural Policy

The end of the 1990s was marked by the Jubilee Debt Campaign, which could be considered the first major success of Minister Wieczorek-Zeul in its practical implementation and was adopted by the heads of state and government of the G8 at the Cologne G8 Summit in June 1999. For debt relief under the HIPC initiative (highly indebted poor countries), (developing) countries could qualify which had received loans from the World Bank exclusively on the most favourable terms. They had to have a debt level of at least 150% of export revenues or more than 250% of government revenues. As part of the initiative, all debts above the aforementioned limits were cancelled by the World Bank after certain conditions were met. The aim of this debt relief was to combat poverty in the affected countries, as the World Bank assumed that the freed-up financial leeway of the countries would be used for domestic development policy measures.

The goal of awakening an endogenous potential to increase investments in infrastructure or in social and educational tasks through a reduced debt service and to reduce the substantial dependence of the affected countries, however, has mostly not been achieved (Stockmann et al. 2016). Therefore, 6 years later in 2005, the Multilateral Debt Relief Initiative (MDRI) was adopted at the G8 Summit in Gleneagles, and noticeable changes occurred in the affected countries. Despite positive examples of the HIPC initiative such as in Ghana, the principle remained that a one-off effect such as a one-time debt relief cannot be a development policy solution for a structural problem, and the debt issue remained a topic of German state development cooperation, albeit to a lesser extent (Kaiser 2019).

Closely linked to the debt relief discussion is also the symbolic role of the so-called Utstein Group. Together with the Norwegian Hilde Johnson, the Dutch Eveline Herfkens and the British Clare Short, Heidemarie Wieczorek-Zeul founded the Utstein Group in 1999 and named it after a monastery in Norway. The four politicians were all development ministers at the time, and the decision to forgive the debts of the poorest of the poor countries is one of their successes. It is even more symbolically relevant in addition to the fact that four women shaped the relevant policies of traditionally strong donor countries in development policy and proved that it is possible to initiate positive changes across party and national borders through close cooperation (Bohnet 2015). The basic conviction was that, on the one hand, development policy should be understood as a cross-cutting task and, on the other hand, all developed countries should make joint and coordinated efforts (Stockmann et al. 2016).

In these years of the so-called Utstein women, strong overlaps of the BMZ with civil society were made on a German level (Bohnet 2015). Initiatives were launched and deepened. Previously, the relationship of the BMZ with associations, churches and non-governmental actors was rather loose and party-politically organised, but now there were approaches to the institutionalisation of contacts and mutual formats for coordination and clarification—be it in Germany within the framework of development policy education and lobbying work as well as in the partner countries of German development cooperation (Roxin et al. 2015).

The professionalisation of the development policy civil society in Germany can be determined, among other things, by the relationship of the BMZ with non-governmental organisations—thus, in 1995, during the time of Minister Spranger, VENRO, the Association for Development Policy and Humanitarian Aid of German Non-Governmental Organisations e.V., was founded as an umbrella organisation of development policy non-governmental organisations in Germany. In 1999, under Minister Wieczorek-Zeul, the Central Peace Service followed as a non-governmental or semi-governmental instrument in the design of development cooperation. As a prehistory, a Berlin Declaration for a Civil Peace Service in Germany was initiated in 1997 under Minister Spranger by numerous civil society groups and personalities from German politics and culture.

As early as 1996, ministerial cooperation and pre-funding took place (Paffenholz et al. 2011). Under the name Consortium Civil Peace Service, the exchange that continues to this day began at the end of 1996 between the participating peace groups and the recognised development services. After the change of government in 1998, the implementation began as a joint project of German peace and development organisations and the BMZ. With public funding the number of partner countries and the approved projects increased while in 1999 the dispatch of the first volunteers happened, whose number also subsequently increased steadily (Vehrenberg 2012; Roxin et al. 2015).

The "Report of the Panel on United Nations Peace Operations", the so-called Brahimi Report (United Nations 2000), recognised failing states as a problem for peace and development in the world and operationalised peace missions as a solution approach (Kühne 2000; Kühne 2001). As a result, approaches to civil-military cooperation were initiated by development cooperation and humanitarian aid and applied primarily in Kosovo but also in other areas with UN peace missions. With the result of the International Commission on Intervention and State Sovereignty (ICISS) "The Responsibility to Protect", a concrete set of rules for humanitarian interventions was adopted, which in the course of the next years also influenced the state development cooperation and its processes (Evans 2008).

On a global level, the Doha Development Round of the WTO—founded as a neoliberal counterpart to UNCTAD in 1995—began in 2001 and put the development problems in many countries of the Global South at the centre of the negotiations. The systemic problems in the Doha Round quickly became apparent, and by 2020 this round despite several adjustments and reforms is not completed (Liebig 2002; Brandi and Helble 2011; Ellmers 2020).

In terms of development policy and contemporary history, the terrorist attacks of 11 September 2001 were a turning point—even more strongly but differently than before, development policy issues were now linked with security policy issues and objectives, leading to a further increase in the politicisation of development cooperation and specifically to the military intervention with subsequent civil reconstruction in Afghanistan.

Development policy gained, in public perception as well as in the political arena in this context additionally, a preventive function in the fight against terrorism (Zürcher et al. 2010; Nachtwei 2011). Thus, the National Security Strategy 2002 of the USA named rogue states, proliferation of weapons of mass destruction and international terrorism as new threats from the Global South—a tendency that led to the Iraq War in 2003.

Here, Germany opposed an intervention, which was then carried out by the USA as a coalition of the willing. The German "no" to the intervention led to an increased reputation of German organisations and development cooperation projects, especially in the African and Arab regions.

After the turn of the millennium, the so-called anchor country concept became increasingly important in German state development cooperation, as the question arose for development policy in general of a stronger systematisation and structuring of development aid and development cooperation beyond national political interests and traditions of the rich (donor) countries of the so-called First World in order to achieve the Millennium Goals (Stamm 2004). For the emerging discourse on how Germany should position itself in its donor role, the German Institute for Development Policy was commissioned as a think-tank with a study on policy advice that should have important recommendations for the self-understanding and the future design of German state development policy:

> Anchor countries are countries that have an outstanding economic and political significance in their respective regional context. This can be positive in the sense of a regional locomotive function or negative in the sense of cross-border stagnation or crisis susceptibility. It

arises from economic interconnections with other countries and from their special importance for regional integration processes and partly from less tangible role model functions. A number of anchor countries are increasingly confidently and actively intervening in international economic and political affairs, playing an important role in the further development of global governance structures. (Stamm 2004, 7)

In addition to the general classification into global governance structures, specific country examples were also named, which should subsequently have effects on the foreign and development policy design of the relations between Germany and the countries:

> It is recommended to designate the countries China, India, Indonesia, Pakistan, Thailand, Egypt, Iran, Saudi Arabia, Nigeria, South Africa, Argentina, Brazil, Mexico as well as Russia and Turkey as anchor countries. Emerging countries are countries that have achieved an above-average level of human development and have the competitive conditions to maintain or further expand this level of development in the future. They usually have consolidated democratic structures and open political systems. It is recommended to designate the countries Chile, Costa Rica, Brazil, Uruguay, Mexico and Mauritius as well as – with certain restrictions – Malaysia and Trinidad & Tobago as emerging countries. (Stamm 2004, 7)

This summary of the classification of countries of the Global South into anchor and emerging countries represented an attempt to sustainably change the design of German development cooperation and above all to take into account the changed global structures, which should also account for different speeds of development of individual states (Klingebiel 2013).

Thus, around the turn of the millennium, the discussion about the growing international influence of some developing countries such as emerging countries increased significantly. Primarily these were China and India, but also Brazil, Indonesia, Mexico and South Africa have since gained a greater global significance due to their economic development and relative political stability, when it came to answering the question of overcoming regional and global challenges in the context of security, trade, climate protection and the regulation of international financial markets.

This assessment was already shared in 2001 by an article from Goldman Sachs beyond the classic development policy, and the acronym BRICS was created and—including Russia—an important factor in shaping international cooperation and development policy was named (O'Neill 2001).

For German state development cooperation, therefore, multilateral development cooperation with its instruments and requirements became increasingly important. Therefore, many new subject areas had to be in the BMZ—also in demarcation or cooperation with other departments and against the backdrop of achieving the MDGs (van de Sand 2004). Moreover, there was also a stronger internationalisation in the other involved departments at federal level, which was reflected in the establishment of sectoral and global competence areas with ODA relevance primarily in the BMBF, BMU, BMWi, BMVg and Chancellery (Bohnet 2017).

One of the most powerful theses of that time is located in the field of environmental and climate protection and focuses on the important role of China and India in the context of global reduction of greenhouse gases (Bohnet 2015). The Brazilian government has also been significantly involved in the issue of tropical protection. As the ongoing regular failure of the Doha Round shows (Brandi and Helble 2011; Frein and Reichert 2012), a number of developing countries in the negotiations on global free trade were united against the positions of the OECD countries and therefore demand the explicit consideration of the interests of these developing countries.

> In many cases, they are also of great importance for the political development of the region. They represent the interests of the region in international forums, they play a central role in regional integration processes (e.g. Brazil in Mercosur) and subcontinental initiatives (Nigeria and South Africa in relation to NEPAD); they often have a guiding and pioneering function towards neighbouring countries (Mexico). As the example of the India, Brazil and South Africa Dialogue Forum [...] shows, anchor countries are beginning to coordinate their actions in the global space and to intensify bi- and trilateral relations. Anchor countries are therefore important partners in international policy dialogue and for future cooperation in global institutions such as the World Bank, the International Monetary Fund, the WTO etc. (Stamm 2004, 20)

The regional relevance of countries such as India, Indonesia, Russia and South Africa for a stable security structure in South Asia and Africa has also become increasingly important, although these countries have not become the hoped-for guarantors of stability and are themselves responsible for many crises still ongoing in 2020 in their regional neighbourhood. The question of how to deal with countries like India and Brazil, which on the one hand are characterised by large socio-economic disparities such as poverty and lack of basic needs security for large parts of the population but on the other hand have become more confident due to their dynamic economy and their political growth in relation to the measures of traditional development cooperation, has been one of the core questions for the design and implementation of state development cooperation since the noticeable globalisation and own development trends of these countries since the mid-2000s (Klingebiel 2013).

This is not a purely German problem; at the latest since the global financial and economic crisis from 2007 to 2009 and the subsequent Euro crisis from 2010 to 2012, new donors—mostly from the circle of countries defined as anchor countries in 2004—have become active. The classic example here is the growing economic and political relations between various sub-Saharan African countries and the People's Republic of China. The substantially increased commitment of the People's Republic of China in the world's poorest region since the mid-2000s means geostrategically and practically that the binding of Western development policy to political and economic reforms was attacked, as the Chinese government did not and does not impose such conditions for international cooperation.

The recommendations of the original anchor country concept were therefore mostly only implemented in German state development cooperation—a strategic reorientation of German foreign policy, which was traditionally focused on Europe and the relationship with the USA, did not take place. Other forms of partnership were also only implemented to a small extent, as the Afghanistan conflict as well as the conflict in Iraq dominated the foreign policy discussion in the media, and in the wake of globalisation, development policy was more focused on poverty reduction and climate transformation and its strategic approaches developed gradually (Klingebiel 2013):

> Given the economic performance of most anchor countries, financial cooperation with a high grant component is usually no longer justified. However, there are novel financing instruments available, in which public funds are only used to a limited extent. They should come into play when they significantly increase the attractiveness of the German offer and increase the significance of the German contribution. Development cooperation with smaller emerging countries can hardly be justified with the aim of overcoming their internal development problems. Wherever possible, other forms of partnership, such as university cooperation or joint projects in the field of environmental research, should take their place. This is increasingly desired by the emerging countries themselves. At the same time, it should be examined how the competencies and grown relationships of development cooperation with actors in these countries can be used to accelerate development processes in poorer countries of the respective region. (Stamm 2004, 8)

The country list of partners of German governmental development cooperation in 2009—at the end of the term of office of Minister Wieczorek-Zeul—includes China as prominently represented as the other anchor countries; a regional focus or functional differentiation according to sectors or policy fields is also not recognisable.

Organisationally, the German governmental development cooperation was shaped by the organisational (partial) concentration of implementing organisations that began in 2002. Under the motto "From Five to Four", the merger of DSE and CDG led to the following restructuring to InWEnt (Popp 2003). The original field of activity of both organisations has been the personnel cooperation with selected partner countries and the aim of intercultural learning from each other (Bühler 1999; Adelmann 1999). This common intersection of activities was with the aim of organisational bundling of the task of qualification, training and further education of specialists and executives from various countries of origin both from countries of the Global North (primarily in the Transatlantic Programme) and the Global South (primarily in the ILT—International Leadership Training) and their institutions merged into a new organisation.

The partners of these InWEnt programmes came from business, politics, administration and civil society. The training of specialists and executives from partner countries always aimed to convey a positive image of Germany and was an important part of the work with partner countries, as most participants from countries of the Global South were also active in development policy relevant sectors of their home countries. Therefore, the ILT was considered an important component of governmental development cooperation:

> The ILT is currently the most important instrument of InWEnt, its costs amount to around 21.5 million euros per year, about 20 percent of the annual InWEnt funding by the BMZ. In international comparison, the ILT is characterised by being more long-term and more practice oriented. (Raetzell et al. 2010, 3)

In the 8 years of its existence, InWEnt therefore always had a special function, which in the German actor landscape of development cooperation clearly differed from the instruments and also the self-understanding of the DED or the

GTZ. Therefore, the merger between CDG and DSE to InWEnt is also certainly to be assessed differently than the later described merger of DED, GTZ and InWEnt to GIZ and the failed reform process of a merger of GIZ with the KfW Development Bank, with the aim of bundling technical and financial cooperation:

> The positive results of the evaluation in terms of development policy relevance, effectiveness and sustainability of the ILT format are pleasing from the BMZ's point of view. The strength of the ILTs lies primarily at the individual level: Almost all participants have benefited significantly from their further training; half of them apply these competencies in around their organisations. The critical assessment of complementarity reveals deficits in the "development cooperation from a single source" and emphasises the necessity of the pre-field reform sought by the BMZ in technical cooperation. By abolishing the institutional boundary between InWEnt and GTZ instruments and through the availability of an external structure for today's InWEnt work, these problems will largely be solved. (Raetzell et al. 2010, 8)

Even after the merger to form GIZ, the ILT instrument was adopted and further developed in a modernisation and adaptation process. An important part of InWEnt was the Service Centre for Municipalities in the One World, a joint facility of the federal government, states and non-governmental organisations to strengthen municipal development cooperation, which in the framework after the World Conference of Rio 1992, but even more so after the follow-up conference of Johannesburg 2002, gradually became an immensely important part of the state development cooperation.

The last years of Wieczorek-Zeul's term of office were characterised by the special role of Germany in the Afghanistan conflict (Zürcher et al. 2010; Nachtwei 2011; Wilson and Kirsch 2014) as well as the discussion about the effectiveness of development cooperation within the framework of the Paris Declaration 2005 and the Accra Action Plan 2008.

In addition to the merger of CDG and DSE to form InWEnt, the establishment and conception of development policy in Germany was marked by the foundation of the volunteer service "weltwärts" as an important milestone (Stern et al. 2011; Blome and Priller 2013). Starting from the then low awareness of many—especially young—people for North-South relations as well as a low acceptance of development policy in general and the willingness to learn globally in particular, there was already the idea of a development policy volunteer service analogous to the civil service or the Voluntary Social Year or Voluntary Ecological Year (Molitor 2012).

There was—due to globalisation and starting from the MDGs and the accompanying question of new global partnerships—a keen interest in a service in countries of the Global South. Especially young people increasingly expressed to carriers of the Voluntary Social Year the interest after their school or training time to do a volunteer service in a country of the Global South. The possibilities of existing offers were usually too expensive, as there was no specially adapted funding for these target countries existed. This was to change with the foundation of "weltwärts":

> Therefore, in 2007, the BMZ introduced the development policy volunteer service "weltwärts". It is intended to take into account the interests of young people in a development policy commitment and at the same time make an effective contribution to development in

the host countries as well as to development policy domestic and educational work in Germany. "weltwärts" is implemented via a wide range of sending organisations, which have partly long-standing cooperations with their partner organisations. The volunteers work in development projects of the local partner organisations. (Stern et al. 2011, 2).

After an evaluation in 2010, the programme was adapted and not—as feared—discontinued under Minister Niebel. The aspect of a North-South exchange with a focus on the joint intercultural and global learning of the participants as well as the involvement of partners from the global South in the sending and partner organisations has since been increasing. The biggest difference to other state and non-state services is that "weltwärts" does not require specialist knowledge in the areas of deployment. It was never designed as a specialist service and thus distinguishes itself as an independent programme—now supervised by Engagement Global—from the specialist services such as the ZFD.

Since 2013, the exchange is no longer one-sided from the Global North as sender to the Global South as partner, but it is both in the North-South and South-North conception. Since 2012, "weltwärts" has been organised as a joint venture between the state and civil society. This means specifically that all actors involved in the voluntary service can and should actively contribute to the design and further development of the implementation and quality assurance of the programme (Stern et al. 2011; Stockmann et al. 2016; Haas and Richter 2019).

The ministerial change to Dirk Niebel as the responsible person can therefore be described as a change in the type of personal appearance, self-understanding as a minister and also the technical objectives of the BMZ. These 4 years are often technically associated with a focus on development financing, the strengthening of development partnerships with the economy, an increase in private-public partnerships and a strengthened private sector development in developing countries and Niebel as an economy-friendly doer who has achieved the long-awaited organisational reform of the implementing organisations (Bohnet 2015).

However, this supposedly economy-friendly development cooperation is based on long preparatory work—the topic of development partnerships with the economy was already a hotly debated topic in 2002/2003 (Altenburg and Chahoud 2002; Altenburg and Chahoud 2003; Blank 2003). In addition, the debate on the importance of foreign economic interests in development cooperation was already controversial and sometimes heated during the times of Erhard Eppler. The "Aid-for-Trade" approach of a stronger linkage between development cooperation and trade policy was discussed and implemented, but the conception of a German trade-related development policy remained one topic among many in the portfolio of development policy implementations (Voionmaa and Brüntrup 2010).

During this time, a lot could also be theorised about the development and foreign policy-shaping power of the FDP, because the role of the FDP-led natural "partner" ministries AA and BMWi in inter-ministerial coordination was relevant in many policy areas, although not as much as many outsiders had hoped. Development policy remained—just like with his predecessor – rather a niche topic compared to the seemingly big foreign and economic policy issues (Bohnet 2015). Important impulses were set, among other things, in health policy, which was achieved through the linkage of medical care, reduction of child and maternal mortality and vaccination programmes in countries of the Global South through multilateral actors and institutions. However, in other policy fields, development policy recommendations or experiences were rather ignored or instrumentalised and overshadowed by foreign and security policy interests.

In addition to the already mentioned country focus on Afghanistan, the German non-participation in the military operation in Libya in 2011 can be cited. A coordination between AA and BMZ took place at least in parts in the newly formulated Africa strategy, a beginning focus of the regional focus of the BMZ, which beyond the federal government was also initiated by the former Federal President Horst Köhler until his resignation (BMZ and AA 2012). However, the focus of German state development cooperation was primarily bilateral; this was internationally reflected by a targeted reduction of the share of multilateral development cooperation from 41.2% to 33.4% (terre des hommes and Welthungerhilfe 2013) and in a departure from budget aid in favour of classic bilateral project and programme financing. Furthermore, contrary to many announcements, the absolute number of projects and partner countries in the period 2009–2013 was hardly or not at all reduced (terre des hommes and Welthungerhilfe 2013).

Dominant was still—and through a stronger linkage with the BMVg—on an intensified level the development policy engagement in Afghanistan, where under the goal of rebuilding democratic structures and securing peace, there was a securitisation of development. This was criticised by many partners from the non-governmental development cooperation community and thus was seen as a fall from grace. Against the backdrop of heavy fighting and an intensity of conflict, the role of German governmental development cooperation was increasingly critically viewed by the involved national actors and later thoroughly evaluated, while other German departments did not do this and the Afghanistan deployment of German state actors in the civilian, military and civil-military sector is still little processed to this day (Nachtwei 2011):

> As of the beginning of 2014, German government funds for development cooperation in Afghanistan amounted to more than 2 billion euros, with the contribution of the Federal Ministry for Economic Cooperation and Development (BMZ) being 1.575 billion euros. Afghanistan is the main recipient of bilateral services through the BMZ. The prominent position of this partner country requires continuous observation. […] The priorities of German development cooperation in Afghanistan have shifted over time. While a quarter of the BMZ portfolio originally focused on emergency aid, this focus shifted towards longer-term development policy goals and longer project durations. To implement this, the BMZ mainly relies on GIZ and KfW as well as some non-governmental organisations on the ground. (Wilson and Kirsch 2014, 6).

In the context of the long focus on development cooperation in Afghanistan, the recommendations for the continuation of cooperation are interesting to read; especially important is the critical self-view and analysis in emphasising the security situation and the important question of the goals of cooperation and the limits of feasibility in fragile contexts:

The reasons for the limited reach and low ambitions of most evaluations are paradoxically found in the high attention that the German mission in Afghanistan enjoys in the German public, as well as in the different objectives, approaches and operational procedures of the five active German ministries and in the security situation in the country. The high attention for the German commitment in Afghanistan puts the actors on the ground under pressure, according to their own statements, to report continuous progress and quick successes. In order to satisfy the constant information needs of the German media, the Bundestag and the government, and also due to the undeniable difficulty of generating secured information about economic and social effects in unstable conditions, the focus of the monitoring and evaluation (M&E) system was even more than usual in international development cooperation on the measurement of delivered services (outputs). (Wilson and Kirsch 2014, 8).

In addition to the commitment in Afghanistan and a slowly developing Africa strategy of the BMZ, the German contribution to the Rio + 20 conference in Rio de Janeiro 2012 is to be seen multilaterally, where specifically the pressing climate and sustainability issues as well as the question of the post-2015 agenda were mainly addressed by countries of the Global South (Repnik 2011). The discussion about the feasibility of "green growth"—a green and sustainable economic growth primarily in countries of the Global South—dominated the global development policy discourse alongside the effectiveness agenda of development cooperation (Messner 2013).

However, this was overshadowed in the media perception in Germany by the management of the Euro crisis, the Euro rescue umbrella, increasing tensions between Russia and the Western world in the context of the Crimea annexation and the rise of the Islamic State in Syria and Iraq following the Syrian civil war and the withdrawal of US troops from Iraq.

Perhaps the greatest development policy legacy during this time, however, is a domestic one. The creation of the GIZ—almost a "from four to two"—with the merger of the DED, the GTZ and InWEnt to form the GIZ with the model of creating a kind of "German aid" in the style of USAID was an important achievement of Minister Niebel. Also, the further tightening and binding of the establishment of the so-called German Houses, where quite practically all German state development actors had the same national Backoffice in a partner country with a single set of logistics and legal basis, is a legacy of this period.. The basic goal of having the external offices of state development cooperation under one roof and one postal address was achieved. The harmonisation, simplification and streamlining of German development cooperation—at least in terms of technical and personnel cooperation—were thus achieved.

A bundling of financial and technical cooperation, i.e. an integration of the KfW Development Bank, did not take place, however. The cabinet decision of 7 October 2010 finally implemented the perhaps biggest reform of development cooperation since the existence of the BMZ in the BMZ's area of responsibility—the merger of GTZ, InWEnt and DED into GIZ (Meyer et al. 2016). In the past, the project of reducing organisational complexity in implementation has failed due to the persistent resistance of individual organisations but also former management of the GTZ or individual politicians. The streamlining of German state development cooperation was a central requirement of the coalition agreement in the field of development policy and was implemented very quickly, effectively and thoroughly within 1 year by the BMZ and the new leadership with Minister Niebel and his State Secretary Beerfeltz. The declared goal of the reform was the increase in political control capacity in development cooperation called for by the OECD (Bohnet 2017):

> The way to achieve this, according to the BMZ's own opinion, is through a clear separation of implementation and political control, which requires a corresponding personnel reinforcement of the BMZ in the new innovative areas. Even the Budget Committee of the German Bundestag welcomed the organisational reform in German development cooperation with its decision of 11 November 2010. It also recognised that a clear separation of implementation and control in development cooperation and personnel strengthening of the BMZ will sustainably improve the political control capacity in this policy area. (Nowak 2012, 75)

In addition to the aspect of increasing political controllability and the signal that organisational success can apparently be dictated by the BMZ through restructurings and mergers, financial reasons were also interesting:

> In total, the merger of the technical implementation organisations of the BMZ (DED, InWEnt, GTZ) into the German Society for International Cooperation (GIZ) saved around 700 positions, according to the BMZ. Even after the further reforms in the realignment of the ministry—such as the creation of a service point for civil society and municipal engagement with almost 145 positions, the creation of an independent evaluation institute with 40 positions and the transfer of positions to the ministry—there is still a reduction in staff or a slimming down of positions in line with the federal budget. (Nowak 2012, 76)

In the aftermath of the merger, Niebel's term of office saw the establishment of Engagement Global gGmbH in January 2012 and in the same year in November the establishment of the German Evaluation Institute for Development Cooperation gGmbH as further state instruments and actors of development cooperation:

> Many of the new topics are [...] already anchored in development policy reality for several years. Nevertheless, not everything in the black-yellow development policy is to be assessed as old wine in new bottles. Rather, the professionalisation of the BMZ and a strong output orientation is something new in state development policy. The greatest formal achievement is certainly the merger of the state implementation organisations into GIZ, but this organisational reform still requires a long breath to really generate efficiency gains in the long term that go beyond simply saving positions in the federal budget. (Nowak 2012, 79).

Above all these domestic and rather organisational milestones of German state development cooperation, however, the shadow of Paris and New York was already looming at the time. This refers first and foremost to the Paris Declaration of 2005, where at the second high-level forum on the effectiveness of development cooperation more than 100 representatives from both donor and partner countries, from international development organisations and from business and civil society agreed on a new agenda that put effectiveness at the centre of their development policy efforts. The following process of the effectiveness agenda of development aid marked the final transition from "aid" to "cooperation" and the sensitisation for partnership cooperation as a standard.

Internationally, the term "assistance" has been used since at least 1961, but it was mostly understood—also in the German context of development policy cooperation—as development aid. The aspect of the claim of a partnership-based equality of donor and recipient countries in the sense of cooperation began as early as the 1990s through the manifold UN world conferences, but it was not until the Paris Declaration and the following conferences in Accra 2008 and Busan 2011 that this was institutionally anchored (Klingebiel 2013).

The core elements of the Accra Action Plan were, on the one hand, the fact that donor countries and partner countries committed themselves emphatically to more transparency, partnership and mutual review and, on the other hand, a division of labour of the donor countries in the sense of harmonisation and strengthening the self-responsibility of the partner countries. This focus of the so-called alignment—the strengthening of self-responsibility and alignment with the priorities of the partner through more consistent use and development of the structures in the partner country—was gradually but steadily established in the structures of state development cooperation after 2008.

In the final declaration of the High-Level Meeting in Busan in 2011, the new partnership for development was finally launched. This addressed the full diversity of donor and recipient structures, so that all global actors in development cooperation—whether industrialised countries, emerging countries or developing countries—together with international development organisations, the private sector and global civil society commit themselves to achieving measurable results in poverty reduction and sustainable development (Klingebiel 2013).

Rio + 20 and the Major Development Conferences: Global Sustainability Policy

But the World Climate Conference 2015 in Paris also cast its shadow long before on the design and formulation of state development cooperation. The aspect of sustainability was increasingly emphasised—so Paris is seen in relation to New York (Stockmann et al. 2016). In New York in 2000, the MDGs were adopted at the Millennium Summit, and a powerful signal was sent for global development—it was also clear that the global successor agenda, the so-called Post-2015 Agenda at the United Nations Summit in New York in September 2015, just over two and a half months before the World Climate Summit in mid-December in Paris, was to be adopted. For this process of creating the Post-2015 Agenda, an open working group within the United Nations system was established in March 2013, which prepared the groundwork for a "future we want" (United Nations 2015a; United Nations 2015b).

Into this development policy environment, Gerd Müller was appointed Minister for Economic Cooperation and Development in 2013. He spent the time until the development policy relevant design year 2015 with a readjustment of the strategic work of the BMZ and a strengthened alignment of the new German development landscape with the merged GIZ, the establishment of Engagement Global for domestic development policy work as well as DEval and also DIE as important impulse givers for a future-oriented development cooperation. A significant focus was certainly the intensified fight against hunger and poverty, also through a linkage with his previous field of action—the BMEL. But the dominant topics should be, besides the all-encompassing orientation towards sustainability, the concentration on the African continent. The claim that development policy is sustainability policy and thus based on a solid foundation of values is an essential claim of his time as minister (Bohnet 2015).

In September 2015, the General Assembly of the United Nations adopted the *Sustainable Development Goals (SDGs)* as part of the 2030 Agenda. These 17 goals, along with their total of 169 sub-goals, set a common framework recognised by all United Nations member states for a desired sustainable development. They effectively replace the *Millennium Development Goals (MDGs)* agreed in September 2000. However, the SDGs are much more than a mere readjustment of the goals set by the MDGs (United Nations 2012). Instead, they testify to a general paradigm shift in the international understanding of development. Although both sets of goals were jointly adopted by all United Nations member states, the focus of the MDGs was primarily on the countries of the Global South. Development here mainly meant combating poverty, hunger and the lack of access to education in countries of the Global South, while the Global North primarily played the role of the "donor", who should finance and implement corresponding projects together with the countries (Debiel 2018).

The SDGs set target specifications that apply to all countries worldwide. The responsibility for adapting national policy to the sustainable target specifications of the United Nations thus lies with all countries, and even the countries of the Global North are in some cases still far from achieving the target specifications (Wege 2023). New is the orientation of the goals towards principles of sustainability, in their social, ecological and economic dimension, and the planetary boundaries, especially in relation to global climate change (United Nations 2015b). This means that the environmental and development agendas of the United Nations, which were previously largely considered separately (Debiel 2018), are summarised in a comprehensive framework programme for sustainable development. When considering goals such as "Reduce inequality within and among countries" (SDG 10), "Ensure sustainable consumption and production patterns" (SDG 12) or "Take immediate action to combat climate change and its impacts" (SDG 13), it becomes clear that achieving the SDGs requires a global socio-ecological transformation (Wege 2023). The underlying question in the implementation of the SDGs, according to Wieczorek-Zeul, is how it will be possible to guarantee sustainable development within the planetary boundaries that creates well-being for all (Wieczorek-Zeul 2017).

The implementation of the SDGs is mainly based on the respective national strategies for sustainable development. In Germany, this takes place in the sustainability strategy of the Federal Government. This strategy, first reissued in 2016 with reference to the SDGs, commits to all 17 SDGs, describes indicators for measuring the implementation of individual SDGs and names their importance for all policy areas.

In addition, it was decided here that a sustainability coordinator should be introduced in each ministry, who will act as the central contact person for the sustainability strategy.

It therefore becomes apparent that the 2030 Agenda and the SDGs at least on paper play an important role for German federal politics in all departments—and thus also in the departments with security responsibility. Especially for the area of German development cooperation under the leadership of the Federal Ministry for Economic Cooperation and Development, a possible redefinition of the concept of development raises interesting questions (Wege 2023).

The relevance of the SDGs for the work of the BMZ is undisputed—also because the BMZ is technically responsible for these in the inter-ministerial work and implementation. Although there is a national-level Secretary of State Committee and close monitoring by the Federal Chancellery, however, the leadership both in the national implementation and in the international, multilateral coordination is led by the BMZ. This is an important political bargaining chip for the head of the BMZ—presently Federal Minister Svenja Schulze—for the (further) design and implementation of sustainable policy in terms of development and beyond.

In the aftermath of the Paris World Climate Conference in 2015 and the subsequent conferences, an emphasis on the ecological triple crisis of climate change, biodiversity loss and environmental pollution in the context of uneven globalisation and existing power asymmetries is certainly guiding for the BMZ. The World Climate Conferences in Glasgow 2021 and later Sharm el-Sheikh 2022 and Dubai 2023 radiate little of the enthusiasm of the World Climate Conference 2015 in Paris and mostly focus on economic consequences. Even a big word like decarbonisation, which was formulated at the G7 summit at Schloss Elmau in 2015 and has flowed into development policy, has not been symbolically located or concretely underpinned since then.

The simultaneity of international crises such as the uncertainty in transatlantic relations under the then US President Trump, the global Corona pandemic, the rise of right-wing populism in almost all Western democracies and the massive increase in irregular migration both to Europe and to the USA as well as within West Africa has a massive influence on the design of German state development cooperation (Ertl 2021; Esteves and Klingebiel 2021). These bundles of crises were reinforced by the geopolitical tensions between Russia and many European states, culminating in the illegal attack by Russia on Ukraine on 24/02/2022, which have made the achievement of global development goals almost impossible (Grävingholt et al. 2023).

In the context of the hasty and chaotic withdrawal of many Western states—and especially Germany—from Afghanistan, the insufficient implementation of the much-vaunted network approach and the insufficient understanding of civil, civil-military and military target corridors became visible (Lipovac and Nowak 2023). A large and important partner country of German development cooperation virtually disappeared overnight from the development policy map and left many open questions regarding the feasibility of development goals in fragile contexts. In summary, by the end of 2021, a failure of many approaches of German development cooperation was being discussed, but at the same time many projects were evaluated and lessons were drawn from the programmes (Gieler 2023).

For a summarising final consideration of this review of more than 30 years of German state development cooperation, reference is made to the concluding quote. The policy field of development policy with all its nuances has long since become a cross-cutting task for modern and humane governance which has an immense and diverse wealth of experience from many actors:

> German development policy has always followed the international paradigm shift from promoting economic growth to satisfying basic needs, supporting structural adjustments and promoting good governance to the Millennium Development Goals and the future sustainability goals. It has considerable conceptual competence and internationally recognised professionalism in implementation. Both have given development policy in the federal government a clear technical independence. It is important to demand and promote the internationally recognised shared responsibility of all policies for global development (policy coherence for development). Competence disputes with the Foreign Office were inevitable but could usually be pragmatically resolved. For some years now, other federal ministries have been engaging with their own financial resources in development cooperation. It is to be hoped that they do not repeat earlier mistakes but use the experiences of the BMZ and the international agreements to improve the effectiveness of development cooperation note. (Ashoff 2014, 2)

References

Adelmann, K. (1999). 40 Jahre DSE. Von der Entkolonialisierung zur Personellen Zusammenarbeit. In: *E+Z 7/8, 40. Jahrgang.* Bonn, 206–211.
Altenburg, T & Chahoud, T. (2002). *Public-Private-Partnership in der Deutschen Entwicklungszusammenarbeit. Synthesebericht.* Bonn.
Altenburg, T & Chahoud, T. (2003). Partnerschaft mit der Wirtschaft – Konsens und Dissens über die weitere Programmgestaltung. In: *E+Z Nr. 6, 44. Jahrgang.* Bonn, 248–249.
Ashoff, G. (2014). Mehr als 60 Jahre deutsche Entwicklungspolitik: noch keine Aussicht auf den Ruhestand. *Deutsches Institut für Entwicklungspolitik (DIE), Die aktuelle Kolumne, 04.09.2014.*
Blank, M. (2003). PPP-Bilanz besser als erwartet. Die ersten Jahre aus Sicht der verfassten Wirtschaft. In: *E+Z Nr. 6, 44. Jahrgang.* Bonn, 244–247.
Blome, C. & Priller, E. (2013). Entwicklungspolitisches bürgerschaftliches Engagement. Ein Beitrag zur Schärfung der Definition. *Discussion Paper SP V 2013-305.* Berlin.
BMZ – Bundesministerium für wirtschaftliche Zusammenarbeit und Entwicklung und AA – Auswärtiges Amt (2012). *Pilotländer zur Stärkung der Außenstruktur im Zuge der Umsetzung der Strukturreform der TZ, Stand: 12.12.2012,* Bonn und Berlin.
Bohnet, M. (2015). *Geschichte der deutschen Entwicklungspolitik. Strategien, Innenansichten, Zeitzeugen, Herausforderungen.* Konstanz.
Bohnet, M. (2017). Politische Ökonomie der deutschen Entwicklungszusammenarbeit. Bestimmungsmuster, Akteure und Allokationsmuster. *DIE Discussion Paper 20/2017.* Bonn.
Brämer, J. & Ziai, A. (2015). Die deutsche Entwicklungspolitik unter Niebel: Eine handlungslogische Analyse des FDP-geführten BMZ. *Peripherie, Nr. 140,* 400–418.
Brandi, C. & Helble, M. (2011). The End of GATT-WTO History? –Reflections on the Future of the Post-Doha World Trade Organization. *DIE Discussion Paper 13/2011.* Bonn.

Bücking, H.-J. (Hrsg.) (1998). *Entwicklungspolitische Zusammenarbeit in der Bundesrepublik Deutschland und der DDR*. Schriftenreihe der Gesellschaft für Deutschlandforschung (GDF), Band 62. Bochum.

Bühler, H. (1999). Wissensvermittlung und Dialog. In: *E+Z 7/8, 40. Jahrgang*. Bonn, 203–205.

Debiel, T. (2018): Entwicklungspolitik in Zeiten der SDGs. Zur Einführung. In: Debiel, T. (Hrsg.). *Entwicklungspolitik in Zeiten der SDGs – Essays zum 80. Geburtstag von Franz Nuscheler*. Duisburg. 5–13.

Ellmers, B. (2020). *Die Finanzierung nachhaltiger Entwicklung in Zeiten von COVID-19 und danach*. Bonn.

Ertl, V. (2021). Die „BMZ 2030"-Reform. Baustein für eine strategische Wirksamkeit der deutschen Entwicklungszusammenarbeit? In: *Auslandsinformationen 2/21 der Konrad-Adenauer-Stiftung*. Berlin. 6–20.

Esteves, P. & Klingebiel, S. (2021). Diffusion, Fusion and Confusion: Development Cooperation in a Multiplex World Order, in: Chaturvedi, S. et al. (Hrsg.): The Palgrave Handbook of Development Cooperation for Achieving the 2030 Agenda. Basingstoke. S. 198–204.

Evans, G. (2008). *The Responsibility to Protect. Ending Mass Atrocities Once and For All*. Washington, D. C.

Frein, M., & Reichert, T. (2012). *Aus der Wüste in die Leere. Die politischen und ökonomischen Gründe für das Scheitern der Doha-Runde der Welthandelsorganisation*. Bonn.

Fukuyama, F. (1992) *The End of History and the Last Man*, New York.

Gieler, W. (2023). Reguliertes Chaos: (Re-)Konstruktionen zum westlichen Ethnozentrismus (2nd ed.). Bonn.

Grävingholt, J., Faust, J., Libman, A., Richter, S., Sasse, G., & Stewart, S. (2023). Wiederaufbau in der Ukraine: Was die internationale Gemeinschaft jetzt beachten muss (*IDOS Policy Brief 2/2023*). Bonn.

Haas, B., & Richter, S. (2019). *Weltwärts im Kontext II: der entwicklungspolitische Freiwilligendienst im Vergleich zu staatlichen Instrumenten der entwicklungspolitischen Bildungsarbeit*. Berlin.

Kaiser, J. (2019). *20 Jahre nach der Schuldenerlass-Initiative der Kölner G8Gipfels – Was wurde aus den HIPCLändern?*. Berlin.

Klingebiel, S. (2013). *Entwicklungszusammenarbeit – Eine Einführung*. Bonn.

Kühne, W. (2000). Friedenseinsätze verbessern – der Brahimi-Report. *SWP-Aktuell, No. 63*. Berlin.

Kühne, W. (2001). Der Brahimi-Report – ein Jahr später. *SWP-Aktuell, No. 13*. Berlin.

Liebig, K. (2002). Quo vadis, WTO? Die Doha-Runde zwischen entwicklungspolitischen Wünschen und politischer Realität. In: *E+Z 8-9, 44. Jahrgang*. Bonn, 324–327.

Lipovac, S. & Nowak, M. (2023). Afghanistan. In: Gieler, W. & Nowak, M. (Hrsg.): *Deutsche Entwicklungszusammenarbeit im Spannungsfeld der Außen- und Sicherheitspolitik: Frieden – Sicherheit – Entwicklung*. Wiesbaden. 265–286.

Messner, D. (2013). Solide Basis. In: *E+Z Nr.7-8*, Bonn, 294–297.

Meyer, L.; Freund, S.; Oltsch, S.; & Polak, J. (2016). *Integration der Instrumente der Technischen Zusammenarbeit*. Deutsches Evaluierungsinstitut der Entwicklungszusammenarbeit (DEval). Bonn.

Molitor, C. (2012). Vom Macher zum Berater. Über den Wandel des Berufsprofils EntwicklungshelferIn, In: *Contacts No. 2/2012*. Köln.

Nachtwei, W. (2011). *The German Mission in Afghanistan: Impact, Results and Consequences*. Berlin.

Niebel, D. (2011). Entwicklungspolitik als Zukunftspolitik, Heidelberger Rede zur Zukunft der deutschen Entwicklungspolitik, Universität Heidelberg, 8. November 2011.

Nowak, M. (2012). Die deutsche Entwicklungspolitik im Umbruch: Eine kritische Betrachtung der von der schwarz-gelben Bundesregierung durchgeführten Maßnahmen. In Zentrum für Niederlande-Studien (Hrsg.), *Jahrbuch/Zentrum für Niederlande-Studien (Band 23)*. Münster, 69–79.

O'Neill, J. (2001). Building Better Global Economic BRICs. *Global Economics Paper No: 66*. New York.

Paffenholz, T., Fino, D., Jütersonke, O., Reimann, S., & Krause, J. (2011). *Der Zivile Friedensdienst. Synthesebericht, Band I: Hauptbericht*. Bonn.

Popp, U. (2003). Dialog und Training weltweit. In: *E+Z 1, 44. Jahrgang*. Bonn, 34–36.

Raetzell, L. et al. (2010). *Das International Leadership Training von InWEnt. Evaluierungsberichte 051*. Bonn.

Repnik, H.-P. (2011). Rio20+ In: *E+Z Nr.12*, Bonn, 468–470.

Roxin, H., Schwedersky, T., Polak, J., Vorwerk, K. & Gaisbauer, F. (2015). *Entwicklungshelferinnen und Entwicklungshelfer*. Deutsches Evaluierungsinstitut der Entwicklungszusammenarbeit (DEval). Bonn.

Stamm, A. (2004). Schwellen- und Ankerländer als Akteure einer globalen Partnerschaft – Überlegungen zu einer Positionsbestimmung aus deutscher entwicklungspolitischer Sicht. *DIE Discussion Paper 01/2004*. Bonn.

Stern, T. et al. (2011). *Der entwicklungspolitische Freiwilligendienst weltwärts. Evaluierungsberichte 056*. Bonn.

Stockmann, R., Menzel, U., & Nuscheler, F. (2016). *Entwicklungspolitik. Theorien – Probleme – Strategien*, 2nd ed., München.

Terre des hommes & Welthungerhilfe (2013): *Die Wirklichkeit der Entwicklungspolitik 2013. Eine kritische Bestandsaufnahme der deutschen Entwicklungszusammenarbeit. Einundzwanzigster Bericht: „Raus aus der Nische! Entwicklungspolitisches Reformprogramm für die neue Bundesregierung"*. Bonn.

Thiel, R. E. (Hrsg.) (2001). *Neue Ansätze zur Entwicklungstheorie*, Bonn.

United Nations (2000). *Report of the Panel on United Nations Peace Operations*. A/55/305, S/2000/809. New York.

United Nations (2012). *The future we want*. Resolution adopted by the General Assembly on 27 July 2012. New York.

United Nations (2015a). *Millenniumsentwicklungsziele Bericht 2015*. New York

United Nations (2015b). *Transforming our world: the 2030 Agenda for Sustainable Development*. Resolution adopted by the General Assembly on 25 September 2015. New York.

Van de Sand, K. (2004). Der Bezugsrahmen ist international verbindlich. In: *E+Z 12/2004, 45. Jahrgang*, Bonn, 470–473.

Vehrenberg, M. (2012). Aktuelle Herausforderungen im Zivilen Friedensdienst. Erfahrungen aus der Praxis gewaltfreier Konfliktbearbeitung. In: *Amosinternational, Jg. 6, Nr. 2*, 11–18.

Voionmaa, P. & Brüntrup, M. (2010). Chancen nutzen. In: *E+Z Nr. 11*, Bonn, 426–427.

Wege, S. (2023). Sicherheitspolitik in den SDGs. In: Gieler, W. & Nowak, M. (Hrsg.): *Deutsche Entwicklungszusammenarbeit im Spannungsfeld der Außen- und Sicherheitspolitik: Frieden – Sicherheit – Entwicklung*. Wiesbaden. 97–114.

Wieczorek-Zeul, H. (2017). Entwicklungspolitik im 21. Jahrhundert. Die Sustainable Development Goals. In: Burchardt, H.-J., Peters, S., Weinmann, N. (Hrsg.): *Entwicklungstheorie von heute – Entwicklungspolitik von morgen*. Baden-Baden. 49–58.

Wilson, M., & Kirsch, R. (2014). *Ein Review der Evaluierungsarbeit zur deutschen Entwicklungszusammenarbeit in Afghanistan*. Deutsches Evaluierungsinstitut der Entwicklungszusammenarbeit (DEval). Bonn.

Woyke, W. (2016). *Weltpolitik im Wandel*. Wiesbaden.

Zürcher, C., Koehler, J., & Böhnke, J. (2010). *Assessing the Impact of Development Cooperation in North East Afghanistan 2005–2009 Final Report*. Bonn.

Chapter 5
German State Development Cooperation in and with Fragile States

Meik Nowak

Abstract To pave the way for a country's development, actors in development cooperation rely on the establishment of a functioning nation-state—because only in this context can bilateral and legally binding agreements ultimately be concluded. If one tries to break out of this ethnocentric perspective, the question arises whether the idea of the developing nation-state is practically applicable everywhere. Can pacification and democratisation in the case of wars and conflicts be achieved from the outside? And if so, how can "failed states" occur? This article deals with the German approach to engagement in fragile states and highlights the importance of the SDGs in this endeavour of German state development cooperation.

Definition of Development Cooperation in Distinction to Humanitarian Aid

Ultimately, numerous state actors provide a form of development cooperation in countries with fragile or weak statehood using different approaches (BMZ 2013; Gieler and Nowak 2021). Since this takes place in a state context, it is rule-based and usually bilateral. Bilateral means that the content, scope and design of development cooperation are institutionalised in some form between the donor and recipient country. Representatives of the two states usually meet for government negotiations or consultations, which generally take place in the recipient country and are integrated on the German side into corresponding country strategies, portfolio strategies and programme plans. The aim of these regular—usually biennial—meetings is the joint assessment of what has been achieved so far, the continuation of the state dialogue and the decision on the future priorities of German engagement

M. Nowak (✉)
Geistes- und Sozialwissenschaften, Helmut-Schmidt-Universität, Hamburg, Hamburg, Germany
e-mail: nowakme@hsu-hh.de

in the recipient country. The new commitments that then arise are legally agreed upon through bilateral agreements. The volume of funds is based on the funds allocated in the federal budget to the individual plan of the BMZ and the medium-term financial planning of the ministry (Gieler and Nowak 2021).

However, every form of state development cooperation usually has one characteristic in common. It comes from state implementation organisations from outside to provide a form of engagement in a country that, in their view, is underdeveloped. There is broad consensus in the assumption that peace is a prerequisite for development (BMZ 2013; Ischinger 2016; BMZ 2018a; Gönner 2022). According to Western understanding, this in turn is only possible in a functioning state with a defined state territory, state people and state power (Barnett and Zürcher 2009; Gieler 2023).

The basic principle of development cooperation is help for self-help. Development cooperation is characterised in its conception and basic understanding by development orientation and structure formation (Wencker and Verspohl 2019). Measures are considered structure-forming from the perspective of development cooperation when institutions and infrastructure are built and strengthened in such a way that they can have their intended effect in the long term even without further external—mostly international—financial and technical support measures (Gieler and Nowak 2021).

Development cooperation creates quickly visible structures in crisis and conflict countries, especially with the approach of transitional aid, e.g. in the areas of food security, health, income or infrastructure. In German development cooperation, the international consensus that has existed since at least 2016 has prevailed that development cooperation can and should also make its contribution in crisis situations. At the World Humanitarian Summit (WHS) 2016 in Istanbul, the then federal government pledged that the artificial separation between humanitarian aid from the budget of the Foreign Office and development cooperation from the BMZ budget is being softened and transitional aid is given a binding framework. In addition to the classic, more long-term and structure-building measures, German development cooperation also has a short- and medium-term effective instrument for achieving its goals. This instrument provides valuable support and a significant contribution to the stabilisation of fragile states (Südhoff and Milasiute 2021).

The publication of the strategy for structure-building transitional aid in July 2020 by the BMZ and the subsequent discussion (BMZ 2020c, 2021) as well as the intensified examination of the principles of humanitarian aid (Hövelmann 2020) located and consolidated the topic. Another factor in the debate was certainly the COVID-19 pandemic, which from 2020 to 2022 at the implementation level led to a strong emphasis on transitional aid and thus to a softening of a rigid project logic in practice.

One consequence of this softening was and is, of course, that now related to various thematic fields similar measures are being carried out—albeit in different contexts, with different partners, but similar in their logic of impact. Thus, even before the COVID-19 pandemic in the field of education, among other things in Afghanistan, Lebanon or Iraq, both the Foreign Office and the BMZ repaired school buildings or financed teacher salaries. In the field of nutrition, vouchers for food were distributed, or there were technical and professional support measures in the context of agricultural production. The German commitment in Afghanistan in its last years until the victory of the Taliban was not clearly distinguishable—according to the then concept of the "networked approach" and civil-military cooperation but also logically (Lipovac and Nowak 2023). Ultimately, this thematic overlap is also obvious in multilateral contexts, as both departments promote measures at various United Nations organisations and multilateral development cooperation works according to different criteria than bilateral development cooperation (Gieler and Nowak 2021; Südhoff and Milasiute 2021).

Humanitarian aid, on the other hand, is primarily committed to the four basic principles of humanity, neutrality, impartiality and independence. A classic self-understanding in sudden crises has always been that it is about saving human lives, providing initial care and alleviating acute distress within the framework of immediate aid. The further instruments are emergency aid as a safeguard of vital basic needs in prolonged crises and humanitarian transitional aid as a continuation or supplement of immediate and emergency aid to stabilise the livelihoods of people in the target countries. Humanitarian disaster prevention and humanitarian mine and ordnance clearance round off the needs orientation of humanitarian aid (Hövelmann 2020; Südhoff and Milasiute 2021).

The implementation and design is done in contrast to development cooperation by independent partners, and the aid is not provided through state agencies to the affected people in the target countries. Humanitarian aid has in case of acute emergencies the objective to cover basic needs and ensure their provision, regardless of the cause of the emergency. It is therefore also seen as an instrument of foreign policy (Wencker and Verspohl 2019; Gieler and Nowak 2021; Südhoff and Milasiute 2021).

Work in Fragile Contexts

Internationally, there is no uniform definition of fragile statehood in literature. Basically, those states are considered unstable or fragile where the state actors are not willing or able to fulfil the basic societal functions in the area of security, rule of law, basic social services and legitimacy for individuals or groups (Rotberg 2002). State institutions in fragile states are usually financially, personally and/or technically very weak or threatened by decay. Usually, the population suffers from high poverty, spontaneous violence and political arbitrariness. As fragile states pose a regional and global security risk, it is a basic assumption of the international community to gently work towards an improvement of the situation through support measures. In this context, development cooperation plays an important role through its inherent structure formation (Rupesinghe 1998; Klingebiel 2013; Brown and Grävingholt 2016).

In the understanding of development cooperation as a structuring element, a clear distinction between the concepts of state-building and nation-building is necessary (Gieler 2023). Nation-building is based on cultural identity and internal cohesion and is therefore only achievable by the citizens of a state themselves. State-building is a structural approach and focuses on the change or construction of administration and institutions.

This change can also be brought about by foreign interventions. With a holistic approach, development cooperation should work equally in three different areas: culture, the individual and structure. If only one area is addressed, it leads to an asymmetry and corresponding failures (Anderson 1999; Klingebiel 2015; Gieler 2023).

For a long time, it was common practice to only build the structure of a country according to the model of a Western constitutional state, i.e. to want to democratise a country, without giving enough account to the people and the culture of the country (Rupesinghe 1998; Mehler and Ribaux 2000). Classic security policy differs here from the strategy of peace policy, which tries to circumvent this problem through the "do-no-harm" approach (Anderson 1999). According to the "do-no-harm principle", unintended undesirable consequences of development cooperation should be recognised early, avoided and mitigated be. Especially programmes in crisis situations must be designed sensitively to conflict according to this principle (Mehler and Ribaux 2000). Unintended effects of development cooperation can, for example, be triggered by the appearance of foreign experts and the distribution of resources and in war or tension areas at worst contribute to the escalation of conflicts (Anderson 1999). Afghanistan is a negative example of this.

The pacification of this country has so far—regardless of the withdrawal in summer 2021—failed, among other things because the existing cultural composition and structures with intra-family loyalties and conflicts were ignored (Lipovac and Nowak 2023). However, Afghanistan is not the only state that is considered failed. Also based on various other cases in the context of fragile statehood, it can be substantiated that nation-building is not the same as state-building (Ziaja and Fabra Mata 2010; Brown and Grävingholt 2016).

South Sudan is also considered a failed state. Over decades there were conflicts that culminated in two civil wars. In 2011, South Sudan split from Sudan and declared its independence. The feeling of common belonging, in this case the feeling of nationhood, developed out of the rebellion. Over 70 different population tribes live in the territory of South Sudan. The Dinkas, with 10% of the population, form the largest ethnic group here and held all important positions in the newly founded South Sudan government and public institutions. The remaining 90% of the population were dissatisfied with the state-building, as they were not represented. The once feeling of common belonging dissolved. Various approaches to counteract this failed, as the United Nations as interlocutor was dependent on the existing government of Dinkas. In 2018, a new solution path was adopted by the tribes themselves. Now there should be four presidents and 35 ministers, who are to be broken down according to the size of the population group. This is a new ray of hope to bring about agreement and to bring about an understanding of common belonging again, which is empirically indispensable for nation-building (Fabra Mata and Ziaja 2009).

The example clearly shows that the parallel emergence of a nation and a rule of law is necessary. However, providing assistance in this process is only difficult, especially since state development cooperation always depends on state agencies in the recipient countries, which are often part of the problem, instead of part of the solution (Baxmann 2016; Weinlich 2018).

Fragility in the Context of the SDGs

Particularly for the Federal Ministry for Economic Cooperation and Development (BMZ) and its work on the ground in the recipient countries of German development cooperation, the SDGs and the 2030 Agenda play a direct role. In its strategy paper on the implementation of the 2030 Agenda (BMZ 2018b), the ministry states that sustainability must be the principle of all human actions in economic, ecological, social and cultural terms, as the planet has limits and its resources are finite.

The goal of political action—according to the BMZ—must be to hand over the earth to the next generation at least as intact as we humans have taken it over (BMZ 2018b). References to the SDGs can also be found on the ministry's homepage, and the reference to the 2030 Agenda plays a prominent role in a large part of the ministry's publications (e.g. BMZ 2020a, 2023).

These 17 goals, along with their total of 169 sub-goals, set a common framework recognised by all United Nations member states for a desired sustainable development. They effectively replace the Millennium Development Goals (MDGs) adopted in September 2000. But the SDGs are much more than just a simple readjustment of the goals set by the MDGs (United Nations 2012). Instead, they testify to a general paradigm shift for the international understanding of development and its influence on German state development cooperation (Wege 2023).

Although both sets of goals were jointly adopted by all United Nations member states, the genuine focus of the MDGs was primarily on the countries of the Global South. Development here meant above all, in the sense of the classic, mostly socio-economically shaped, Western understanding of development, the fight against poverty, hunger and lack of access to education in countries of the Global South, while the Global North mainly took on the role of the "donor" who should finance and implement corresponding projects together with the countries (Debiel 2018; Wege 2023).

The issue of "security" was not addressed, nor was the relevance of the aspect of "peace", and was only subtly present in MDG 8 "Creating a global partnership for development". Here, the subtle emphasis on basic human rights was outlined—the right of every person on this planet to health, education, housing and security (Wege 2023). If one looks at the SDGs from the perspective of fragility, a relevant aspect for work in fragile states can be distilled from each SDG (Baxmann 2017). This concerns aspects of environmental migration (Rhyner 2017), demography or dealing with flight and displacement based on wars and conflicts (Dietrich 2018) and is a perspective that is reflected in sectoral and cross-sectoral concepts of German development cooperation or peace work (BMZ 2018a, b, 2020b, c).

For the implementation of the SDGs in state development cooperation with fragile states, the respective national strategies play a major role (Baxmann 2017). In Germany, this takes place primarily in the area of the already mentioned structure-forming transitional aid (BMZ 2020c), as well as in the individual approaches and country strategies of the BMZ in the context of the so-called Triple Nexus between humanitarian aid, development cooperation and peace policy (Hövelmann 2020).

Possible Adjustments of Development Policy to the 2030 Agenda

As Alexandra Rudolph argued in an important development policy contribution as early as 2016, German state development policy would need to adapt in some areas in order to better meet the goals of the 2030 Agenda, especially in the context of changing framework conditions. Specifically, she mentions areas such as the channels of allocation, country selection and sector selection within development cooperation (Rudolph 2016). While she does not explicitly refer to fragility, some important German contributions to the discussion originate from the question of the connection between sustainable development and the SDGs with the project and life reality in countries with fragile statehood in the Global South (Baxmann 2017; Klingebiel 2018).

Rudolph particularly advocates for a stronger focus on multilateral rather than bilateral development cooperation. While bilateral development cooperation has a higher potential to assert one's own donor interests and tie financial resources to measures that do not necessarily have to be in line with the 2030 Agenda, multilateral development cooperation offers a higher degree of transparency and coordination between the various goal levels of the Agenda (Rudolph 2016). At the same time, a stronger focus on multilateral development cooperation would require politicians and implementing organisations of development cooperation to relinquish control over development funds to international organisations, which they are presently still reluctant to do (Rudolph 2016; Weinlich 2018).

Research argues that the United Nations organisations, which are already the largest actors in multilateral development cooperation, have a lot of potential for a consistent embedding of the SDGs in development cooperation. On the one hand, they are attributed a higher legitimacy, impartiality and credibility than other organisations, and, on the other hand, they are well capable of collecting relevant data, supporting states in setting up national strategies and accompanying the negotiation processes between potential goal conflicts (Weinlich 2018).

According to Rudolph, the sectoral focus within a country would also need to be adjusted to reduce the self-interests of the donor countries further in order to give sufficient attention to all SDGs and to do justice to the indivisibility of the individual goals (Rudolph 2016). In particular, sectors such as climate and health need to be given more attention. Individual donors are also hardly able to cover all areas of the SDGs at the same time. Therefore, a departure from a development policy primarily oriented towards donor interests and a strengthening of multilateral institutions is necessary. In addition to better coordination of development cooperation in the interest of all SDGs, a stronger role of multilateral development cooperation would also have the advantage of reducing the number of donor organisations in the partner countries, which would in turn simplify coordination with the country structures (Rudolph 2016; Baxmann 2017).

Rudolph further argues that the type of country selection must be adapted to the goals of the 2030 Agenda. Although SDG 17 clearly states that those countries with the greatest need for international support should be considered (Martens and Obenland 2016), these countries are increasingly receiving less support in practice. This is because supporting the poorest and conflict-affected countries often offers no economic or strategic added value for the donor countries and is therefore often neglected (Rudolph 2016; Weinlich 2018). Here too, the national interests of the financially stronger countries are in conflict with the global goals of the 2030 Agenda.

It thus becomes apparent that while the traditional actors of German development policy like to refer to the goals of the 2030 Agenda in their public relations work and also present their previous work areas in the light of the SDGs, there can hardly be any talk of an SDG-compliant transformation of the sector. Measures such as better evaluating all levels of sustainable development in development cooperation projects, as demanded by DEval (Noltze et al. 2018), would be a step in the right direction. Ultimately, however, the question arises whether a transformation of development cooperation in the sense of the 2030 Agenda does not require a much greater rethink, which goes beyond procurement practices, sectoral priorities or country selection.

As a consequence of the SDGs, the BMZ has been focusing since 2020 on a concentration of development policy issues and thus wants to set new priorities in the spirit of the "Paris Declaration" 2005 and the often criticised High-Level Forum of Busan 2011 in areas such as climate protection, health and family policy, the establishment of sustainable supply chains, the use of digitisation and technology transfer and the strengthening of private investments (BMZ 2023). It is noticeable that the aspect of peace policy and security is not mentioned as a priority. Among the bilateral partner countries, there are noticeably many fragile states—but a special role or even preferential treatment is not apparent. The BMZ's reform concept for country selection from 2020, which was initiated by the previous Minister Müller, was stopped by his successor Schulze and modified towards greater multilateralism. The focus on clear-cut criteria, e.g. based on fragility indicators, only takes place in parts and is aptly summarised by Gieler and Nowak in 2021:

> So what is genuinely "new" about the new reform concept? It is the belated development in relation to the guiding principles of Paris, Accra and Busan – a redesign of partnership criteria and forms of international cooperation beyond political or traditional needs and sensitivities. Thus, new partnership categories are formed to protect global goods such as

climate, biodiversity and human security in conflict and refugee areas, in order to effectively support partner countries (BMZ 2020b). This can also be read as a veiled admission that the traditional instruments of German state development cooperation were not always precise, purposeful and effective in the past. The form and nature of the cooperation of German state actors with the partner countries is also changing. How exactly this happens, the reform concept is still rather nebulous and mixes the value-based argument for a reform with the functional-instrumental argument and clearly states that development cooperation can also be (re)designed according to the "carrot and stick" model. (Gieler and Nowak 2021, p. 311)

The new country concept, however, emphasises a modified list of countries according to partnership categories. These categories, however, only concern German state bilateral development cooperation and not the development cooperation of private carriers, political foundations, civil society and churches. Now, 65 states are grouped into four categories, but only ten states are so-called Nexus and peace partners of Germany. These are seven least developed countries (Afghanistan, Yemen, Democratic Republic of Congo, Somalia, Sudan, South Sudan, Chad) and three middle income countries (Iraq, Libya and Syria). Among other things, the strategic realignment to the 2030 Agenda and the derived SDGs is cited as the reason for the country concept.

But in addition to the integration of ecological, social, economic and cultural dimensions of sustainability into the various areas of the SDGs, the 2030 Agenda also refers to a new understanding of development. As already became clear in the introduction, the SDGs show deficits in terms of sustainable development for all countries—not just for countries of the Global South. A division of the world into "developing countries" and "already developed countries", already a problematic power-political issue before the 2030 Agenda (Ziai 2014), appears even more outdated and paternalistic in the light of the SDGs.

Although countries differ in the extent to which they have already achieved the individual SDGs and the resources available to them to achieve these goals, no country can yet boast of having already completed a development in the sense of the 2030 Agenda—or at least to be on the direct path to it. In this sense, all countries of the world could be described as "developing countries" (Wege 2023). So if the dichotomy between takers and givers, between developing and developed countries, is to be dissolved in the 2030 Agenda, what does this mean for the field of development cooperation?

Even though German development cooperation likes to describe itself as a partnership on an equal footing, Müller and Ziai (2015) argue that it is still characterised by strong hierarchies and Eurocentric worldviews that are firmly anchored in European development policy. The authors distinguish between three levels of asymmetric relationships in development cooperation, namely, hierarchies related to the experts, the donors and the norms in the development context (Müller and Ziai 2015).

With the term expert hierarchy, they describe the assumption underlying a large part of development cooperation that countries of the Global South have the most significant societal problems, while the Global North has the greater problem-solving competencies (Müller and Ziai 2015). The partner structure is thus far from being a communication on an equal footing, in which the countries exchange their expertise without hierarchy. The donor hierarchy, according to Müller and Ziai, refers to the material dependence of the countries of the Global South on the Global North. Due to the different financial power, forms of symbolic dominance and economic neediness would be created. This would enable the countries of the Global North to enforce their idea of "good" development and thus also strengthen their hierarchy of norms. Under this hierarchy of norms, the two authors understand the sum of the Eurocentric value ideas that present the Global North as (further) "developed" and the Global South fundamentally as deficient and in need of help (Müller and Ziai 2015).

Conclusion

The funds for short-term aid increased by the refugee crisis in 2015 and the softening between development cooperation and humanitarian aid decided at the WHS 2016 in Istanbul; there is a strong trend towards a revitalisation of civil conflict resolution. Since 2015, there has been a gigantic increase in funds in German development cooperation and humanitarian aid. Thus, the three titles transitional aid (BMZ), humanitarian aid (AA) and stabilisation (AA) have more than quadrupled to a total of almost 3.3 billion euros in the federal budget 2021 (Gieler and Nowak 2021; Südhoff and Milasiute 2021). How the new BMZ reform and the focus of the new minister will affect this is still completely unclear.

The disruptions caused by the COVID-19 pandemic from 2020 were gigantic, and the resulting changes in the structures on site are not yet fully foreseeable (BMZ 2021). Afghanistan may appear as a particularly clear example of the failure of the Western security and development approach (Lipovac and Nowak 2023)—the disruptions caused by the Russian war of aggression against Ukraine from 24/02/2022 are also a major challenge for German state development cooperation (Grävingholt et al. 2023). Thus, the BMZ is primarily responsible for coordinating the German aid for the Ukrainian state—the "Platform Reconstruction Ukraine" of the federal government is implemented by the BMZ.

Furthermore, the agreed international principles for the reconstruction of Ukraine are also financed via the BMZ. Here, the question arises of a linkage of state development cooperation with security policy interests and also a possible redefinition of the role of the BMZ against the background of the aid provided to the Ukraine (Gönner 2022; Leininger and Hornidge 2024). Besides this particular point, the most exciting question remains to what extent state development cooperation can use the SDGs to stabilise fragile states or help the population living there. Therefore, this article ends with an encouraging quote from Marc Baxmann, which unfortunately has not lost any of its relevance over the years:

As a consequence, development cooperation must become more political. All international engagement in fragile contexts, from planning to implementation, must be specifically aimed at crisis prevention, conflict management and peace promotion in order to achieve the SDGs in fragile states. This requires increased analytical capacities (also on site), innovative instruments, more willingness to take risks and appropriate resource allocation. (Baxmann 2016, p. 4)

References

Anderson, M. (1999). *Do No Harm. How Aid Can Support Peace – Or War*. Boulder.
Barnett, M. & Zürcher, C. (2009). The peacebuilding contract. How external statebuilding reinforces weak statehood. In: R. Paris & T. Sisk (ed.): *The Dilemma of Statebuilding. Confronting the contradiction of postwar peace operations*. London. 23–52.
Baxmann, M. (2016). Die Agenda 2030: Ein Instrument für nachhaltige Entwicklung in fragilen Staaten? *Global Governance Spotlight, No. 4/2016*. Bonn.
Baxmann, M. (2017). Hilfreiches Prinzipienreiten: Wie die Agenda 2030 friedlichen Wandel in Konfliktsituationen ermöglichen kann. *FriEnt Briefing Nr. 12*, Bonn.
BMZ – Bundesministerium für wirtschaftliche Zusammenarbeit und Entwicklung (2013). Entwicklung für Frieden und Sicherheit. Entwicklungspolitisches Engagement im Kontext von Konflikt, Fragilität und Gewalt. *BMZ-Strategiepapier 4/2013*. Bonn & Berlin.
BMZ – Bundesministerium für wirtschaftliche Zusammenarbeit und Entwicklung (2018a). *Entwicklungspolitik ist Zukunftspolitik. Ressortbericht des Bundesministeriums für wirtschaftliche Zusammenarbeit und Entwicklung (BMZ) zur Umsetzung der Deutschen Nachhaltigkeitsstrategie und der SDGs*. Bonn & Berlin.
BMZ – Bundesministerium für wirtschaftliche Zusammenarbeit und Entwicklung (2018b). *Entwicklungspolitik 2030. Neue Herausforderungen – neue Antworten*. BMZ-Strategiepapier. Bonn & Berlin.
BMZ – Bundesministerium für wirtschaftliche Zusammenarbeit und Entwicklung (2020a). *Gemeinsam weiter – Zukunft denken*. Bonn & Berlin.
BMZ – Bundesministerium für wirtschaftliche Zusammenarbeit und Entwicklung (2020b). *Reformkonzept „BMZ 2030" Umdenken – Umsteuern*. Bonn & Berlin.
BMZ – Bundesministerium für wirtschaftliche Zusammenarbeit und Entwicklung (2020c). *Strategie der strukturbildenden Übergangshilfe. Krisen bewältigen, Resilienz stärken, Perspektiven schaffen*. Bonn & Berlin.
BMZ – Bundesministerium für wirtschaftliche Zusammenarbeit und Entwicklung. (2021). *Erfahrungen aus der Praxis des Humanitarian-Development-Peace Nexus: eine Literatursichtung*. Bonn & Berlin.
BMZ – Bundesministerium für wirtschaftliche Zusammenarbeit und Entwicklung (2023). *BMZ-Agenda für gute Arbeit weltweit*. Bonn & Berlin.
Brown, S. & Grävingholt, J. (Hrsg.) (2016). *The securitization of foreign aid*. Basingstoke.
Debiel, T. (2018): Entwicklungspolitik in Zeiten der SDGs. Zur Einführung. In: Debiel, T. (Hrsg.). *Entwicklungspolitik in Zeiten der SDGs – Essays zum 80. Geburtstag von Franz Nuscheler*. Duisburg. 5–13.
Bundesregierung der Bundesrepublik Deutschland (Hrsg.). (2017). *Krisen verhindern, Konflikte bewältigen, Frieden fördern. Leitlinien der Bundesregierung*. Berlin.
Dietrich, I. (2018). Die Agenda 2030 für nachhaltige Entwicklung: Ein Beitrag zur Verringerung von Fluchtursachen? In: Wagner, R. & Schaprian, H.-J. (Hrsg.): *Handlungsfähigkeit stärken – Stabilität schaffen. Überlegungen zur Europäischen Sicherheits- und Verteidigungsunion*. 56–62. Magdeburg.
Fabra Mata, J. / S. Ziaja (2009). *Users' Guide on Measuring Fragility*. Bonn & Oslo

Gieler, W. (2023). *Reguliertes Chaos: (Re-)Konstruktionen zum westlichen Ethnozentrismus* (2nd ed.). Bonn.

Gieler, W. & Nowak, M. (ed.) (2021). *Staatliche Entwicklungszusammenarbeit in Deutschland: Eine Bestandsaufnahme des BMZ 1961–2021*. Wiesbaden.

Gönner, T. (2022). Sicherheit durch Nachhaltigkeit – Vernetzt arbeiten für eine krisenfestere Welt. In: Behörden Spiegel-Gruppe in Zusammenarbeit mit dem Bundesverband der Deutschen Sicherheits- und Verteidigungsindustrie e.V. (BDSV) (Hrsg.): *Frieden, Sicherheit, Nachhaltigkeit – Beiträge zu einer gesellschaftspolitischen Debatte*. Bonn. 30–31.

Grävingholt, J., Faust, J., Libman, A., Richter, S., Sasse, G., & Stewart, S. (2023). Wiederaufbau in der Ukraine: Was die internationale Gemeinschaft jetzt beachten muss (*IDOS Policy Brief 2/2023*). Bonn.

Hövelmann, S. (2020). *Triple Nexus to go: Humanitäre Themen erklärt*. Berlin.

Ischinger, W. (Hrsg.) (2016). *Munich Security Report 2016 – Boundless Crises, Reckless Spoilers, Helpless Guardians*. München.

Klingebiel, S. (2013). Konfliktbewältigung und Umgang mit fragilen Staaten. In: *Aus Politik und Zeitgeschichte (APuZ) 37/2013*, 23–27.

Klingebiel, S. (2015). Zukunft der Entwicklungszusammenarbeit. In: *Aus Politik und Zeitgeschichte (APuZ) 65 (7–9)*, 16–22.

Klingebiel, S. (2018). Entwicklungspolitische Kooperationsansätze in Zeiten der Agenda 2030 & SDGs. Zur Notwendigkeit einer Neubestimmung. In: Debiel, T. (Hrsg.). *Entwicklungspolitik in Zeiten der SDGs – Essays zum 80. Geburtstag von Franz Nuscheler*. Duisburg. 168–171.

Leininger, J. & Hornidge, A. (2024). Sicherheitspolitik ist nicht Entwicklungspolitik (*Die aktuelle Kolumne 19.02.2024*). Bonn.

Lipovac, S. & Nowak, M. (2023). Afghanistan. In: Gieler, W. & Nowak, M. (eds.): *Deutsche Entwicklungszusammenarbeit im Spannungsfeld der Außen- und Sicherheitspolitik: Frieden – Sicherheit – Entwicklung*. Wiesbaden. 265–286.

Martens, J. & Obenland, W. (2016). *Die 2030-Agenda. Globale Zukunftsziele für nachhaltige Entwicklung*. Bonn.

Mehler, A. & Ribaux, C. (2000). *Krisenprävention und Konfliktbearbeitung in der Technischen Zusammenarbeit: Ein Überblick zur nationalen und internationalen Diskussion*. Wiesbaden.

Müller, F. & Ziai, A. (2015). Eurozentrismus in der Entwicklungszusammenarbeit *Aus Politik und Zeitgeschichte (APuZ) 65 (7–9)*, S. 8–15.

Noltze, M., Euler, M., Verspohl, I. (2018). *Meta-Evaluierung von Nachhaltigkeit in der deutschen Entwicklungszusammenarbeit*. Bonn.

Rhyner, J. (2017). Environmental Risks and Human Security in the Context of Global Change. In: Bindenagel, J., Herdegen, M. & Kaiser, K. (Hrsg.): *International Security in the 21st Century – Germany's International Responsibility*, 143–148. Bonn.

Rotberg, R. (2002). Failed States in a World of Terror. In: *Foreign Affairs, Vol. 81, No. 4 (Jul. – Aug., 2002)*, S. 127–140.

Rudolph, A. (2016). *Wie kann Entwicklungszusammenarbeit SDG-sensitiv ausgestaltet werden?* Bonn.

Rupesinghe, K. (1998). *Civil wars, civil peace: An introduction to conflict resolution*. London.

Südhoff, R. & Milasiute, G. (2021). *Zeit für einen Neuanfang? 5 Jahre World Humanitarian Summit und Grand Bargain*. Berlin.

United Nations (2012). *The future we want*. Resolution adopted by the General Assembly on 27 July 2012. New York.

Wege, S. (2023). Sicherheitspolitik in den SDGs. In: Gieler, W. & Nowak, M. (Hrsg.): *Deutsche Entwicklungszusammenarbeit im Spannungsfeld der Außen- und Sicherheitspolitik: Frieden – Sicherheit – Entwicklung*. Wiesbaden. 97–114.

Weinlich, S. (2018). SDGs ernstnehmen: Konsequenzen für das VN-Entwicklungssystem. In: Tobias Debiel (Hrsg.); *Entwicklungspolitik in Zeiten der SDGs: Essays zum 80. Geburtstag von Franz Nuscheler*. Duisburg. 162–167

Wencker, T. & Verspohl, I. (2019). *German Development Cooperation in Fragile Contexts*. German Institute for Development Evaluation (DEval), Bonn.
Ziai, A. (Hrsg.) (2014). *Im Westen nichts Neues? Stand und Perspektiven der Entwicklungstheorie*. Baden-Baden.
Ziaja, S. & Fabra Mata, J. (2010). State Fragility Indices: Potentials, Messages and Limitations. *DIE Briefing Paper 10/2010*. Bonn.

Chapter 6
German Development Cooperation in the Context of the Ukraine Conflict

Wolfgang Gieler and Meik Nowak

Abstract The German state development cooperation in the context of the Ukraine conflict is an increasingly relevant and multifaceted topic. The effects of the conflict on German development cooperation and the associated political and strategic decisions are examined. The challenges and opportunities that Germany faces in providing humanitarian aid, reconstruction and long-term development cooperation in Ukraine and the surrounding regions are analysed. Special attention is given to Germany's diplomatic efforts to shape development cooperation with the aim of stabilising the region and promoting peace and security. The investigation is based on present political developments and the principles of German development cooperation in conflict and crisis areas. Finally, possible future scenarios are outlined, and recommendations for action for German development cooperation in the context of the Ukraine conflict are presented.

Increased Development Aid: Ukraine Conflict's Impact on International Assistance and Refugee Costs

Last year, the approximately 30 members of the Development Assistance Committee (DAC) of the Organisation for Economic Co-operation and Development (OECD) recorded a significant increase in their public development cooperation (Official Development Assistance, ODA) to a total of about 204 billion US dollars. This represents an increase of more than 13% compared to the previous year. This increase

---

W. Gieler (✉)
Sozialwissenschaften, Fachhochschule Dortmund, Dortmund, Nordrhein-Westfalen, Germany
e-mail: wolfgang.gieler@fh-dortmund.de

M. Nowak
Geistes- und Sozialwissenschaften, Helmut-Schmidt-Universität,
Hamburg, Hamburg, Germany
e-mail: nowakme@hsu-hh.de

© The Author(s), under exclusive license to Springer Fachmedien Wiesbaden GmbH, part of Springer Nature 2024
W. Gieler, M. Nowak (eds.), *Understanding German Development Cooperation*, Contributions to Political Science, https://doi.org/10.1007/978-3-658-45596-5_6

is also reflected in the ODA quota which measures the proportion of development funds in the gross national income (GNI) of the donor countries. According to the OECD, the ODA quota increased from 0.33% to 0.36%. Despite this increase, the ODA quota is still significantly below the internationally agreed target value of 0.7% (OECD 2023).

A considerable part of this increase is due to the accommodation of refugees from various parts of the world in the donor countries. These costs can partly be booked as development funds, which led to a total of 29.3 billion dollars or 14.4% of the total development funds being allocated to this area in 2022. This allocation represents a doubling compared to the previous year, when the costs for the accommodation of refugees amounted to just under 13 billion dollars (Zapf et al. 2023).

The significant increase in expenditure for the accommodation of refugees results directly from the war in Ukraine, which has led to a drastic increase in the number of refugees worldwide. The initial escalation of the Ukraine conflict has manifested itself in numerous European states in a clear way, particularly through the considerable increase in Ukrainian refugees, as documented by the United Nations High Commissioner for Refugees (UNHCR) in 2022. This situation has led to a significant increase in asylum costs in the affected countries, with governments and humanitarian organisations facing enormous challenges in meeting the needs of the refugee population. Overall, the drastic increase in expenditure for the accommodation of refugees highlights the immediate effects of the Ukraine conflict on the European states and the need for a coordinated and comprehensive international response to manage the humanitarian crisis and ensure the protection and support of the affected population (UNHCR 2022).

The Russian attack on Ukraine on 24 February 2022 has profound effects not only on the countries directly affected but also on the entire geopolitical situation in Europe and beyond. This invasion represents a blatant violation of fundamental principles of international order and international law and has far-reaching consequences for the stability and security of the entire region.

The immediate consequences of this aggression primarily affect the territorial integrity of Ukraine, which is directly threatened. However, it also destabilises the entire region and raises serious questions about the security and future of Europe. The reactions to this have caused political, economic and social upheavals and shaken the trust between European states.

The international community has responded to this aggression with various measures aimed at protecting the territorial integrity of Ukraine and holding those responsible to account. This has led to a broad discussion about the role of diplomacy, sanctions and other tools for conflict resolution.

To restore long-term stability and security in the region, it is crucial that the international community works together to find a diplomatic solution to the conflict. The principles of sovereignty, independence and territorial integrity must be respected and defended to prevent future aggression and ensure peaceful coexistence (Bliman 2024).

The verbal declarations from the Russian president suggest that further aggressive actions by Russia must be considered, which represents a continuing threat to the region. This ongoing uncertainty contributes to the escalation of tensions and poses a significant challenge to stability and security in Europe. In this extremely complex context, Ukraine not only acts as a defender of its own territory but also as a guarantor for general security and stability in Europe. The country's consistency and determination are of critical importance for maintaining peace and security on the European continent (Urech 2023; BMZ 2023).

Germany's Support and Security Agreement with Ukraine: Tackling Urgent Challenges Amidst Crisis

Considering the serious challenges Ukraine faces, the Federal Government has decided to provide extensive support to Ukraine and conclude a security agreement with it. This decision was made based on a thorough analysis of the present situation and a recognised urgency to take both military and civilian measures to support Ukraine in this difficult time.

The Federal Government's decision reflects the recognition of the serious threats Ukraine is facing, as well as the commitment to provide solidarity support. The comprehensive support and the security agreement are intended to help strengthen Ukrainian security and stability and improve its ability to deal with present challenges. Both military and civilian aspects are considered to cover a broad spectrum of needs and ensure an effective response to the various dimensions of the crisis.

The Federal Government's decision is in line with the principles of international cooperation and solidarity, as well as Germany's legal obligations as a member of the international community. It underscores Germany's willingness to make a constructive contribution to addressing global challenges and supporting partner countries in times of need. These measures demonstrate a strategic approach and an understanding of the complexity of the situation. They underline the Federal Government's determination to take concrete steps to strengthen security and stability while promoting the country's long-term development and prosperity.

German support for Ukraine includes a wide range of measures that go beyond purely military aid. In addition to providing weapons and military equipment, Germany recognises the need to grant Ukraine access to basic resources that are crucial for the country's survival and stabilisation (Federal Government 2024, 3).

Access to electricity plays a fundamental role in the functioning of industry, infrastructure and the daily life of the population. By ensuring a stable power supply, Germany can contribute to improving living conditions in Ukraine and boosting economic development.

A functioning health system is essential to meet the medical needs of the population, especially in times of armed conflict. Germany therefore supports Ukraine in the provision of medical equipment, training of health personnel and the establishment of medical facilities.

Education is a key factor for the future of Ukraine and its population. Germany contributes to improving access to educational institutions, providing teaching materials and promoting the training of teachers to ensure educational opportunities for all population groups. Furthermore, the stability of the economy is crucial to support the reconstruction of the country and lay the foundations for sustainable development. Germany offers support in economic stabilisation and reforms to assist Ukraine on its path to a stable and prosperous future (Grävingholt et al. 2023).

The provision of these basic resources is of utmost importance to meet the urgent challenges of war and effectively manage reconstruction. Through comprehensive support at various levels, Germany can contribute to promoting the long-term stability and development of the country and contribute to the security and prosperity of the entire region. The provision of these civilian aid measures is not only a moral obligation but also crucial for the security and stability in Europe. A stable and economically prosperous Ukraine will contribute to ensuring long-term security in the entire region and contain potential threats.

The security agreement between Germany and Ukraine marks an important step towards a comprehensive partnership to address present challenges. It demonstrates the commitment of both countries to promoting peace, security and prosperity in the region and beyond. It is crucial that these measures are accompanied by a coordinated international effort to find a sustainable solution to the crisis and ensure long-term stability in the region. Only through a joint effort of the international community can the challenges facing Ukraine be effectively addressed (Federal Government 2024, 3).

German Development Cooperation: Supporting Ukraine's Path to Stability and Prosperity

Given the present warlike events, German state development cooperation plays an essential role in supporting and strengthening Ukraine. A primary goal is to promote the economic stability of the country, especially against the backdrop of instability caused by the conflict. This involves both short-term measures for economic stabilisation and long-term strategies for sustainable growth and development.

Another focus is on promoting transparent government structures to combat corruption and strengthen democratic institutions. The establishment of transparent and accountable government practices is intended to strengthen the population's trust in the government and improve the efficiency of public administration.

In addition, German development cooperation actively supports the establishment of a democratic society in Ukraine by promoting civil rights, freedom of expression and democratic processes. Civil society organisations and democratic actors are supported in establishing a diverse and strong democratic structure.

Another important aim is to guide the country on its path to becoming an integral part of Europe, with the possibility of opening prospects for EU accession. This includes promoting reforms that facilitate alignment with European norms and standards, as well as supporting the country's integration into European structures. Through a wide range of measures, German development cooperation aims to integrate Ukraine into the European community in the long term and to enable it a stable and prosperous future (BMZ 2023).

The Federal Ministry for Economic Cooperation and Development (BMZ) has responded quickly and efficiently to the start of the Russian war of aggression against Ukraine. Since February 2022, the BMZ has provided around 1.2 billion euros to support Ukraine. Initially, the aid focused on the implementation of support programmes. However, these are now gradually being replaced by long-term strategies aimed at promoting the reconstruction of the country as a priority. In doing so, the BMZ can draw on established partnerships and a wealth of experience from around two decades of development cooperation with Ukraine.

The implementation of the planned projects is primarily carried out by the German Society for International Cooperation (GIZ) and the Kreditanstalt für Wiederaufbau (KfW), in close cooperation with the European Union, the United Nations and the World Bank. In addition to these institutions, municipal partnership work and cooperation with civil society play a significant role in this context (BMZ 2023).

Development policy cooperation also extends to a large number of other international organisations, including the United Nations Children's Fund (UNICEF), the International Organisation for Migration (IOM), UN Women, the United Nations Human Settlements Programme (UN-Habitat), the United Nations Development Programme (UNDP), the World Food Programme (WFP) and the Economic Commission for Europe (UNECE). Through targeted projects and increasing voluntary core contributions, the Federal Government enables these organisations to continue their ongoing programmes and activities in Ukraine and the region and to respond quickly.

Exemplary measures in cities such as Kharkiv and Mykolaiv are supported by UNECE and local authorities to promote citizen-friendly and sustainable reconstruction. The financing of the UNICEF education fund "Education Cannot Wait" ensures safe learning and psychosocial support for children and young people. Furthermore, funds are provided for UNDP to maintain the Ukrainian government's emergency management, and UN Women is supported in providing information and advice on the specific needs of Ukrainian women and girls (BMZ 2023).

Overall, German development cooperation aims to comprehensively support and strengthen Ukraine. Through the successful implementation of these goals, Germany wants to make a significant contribution to the long-term stability, development and integration of Ukraine, as well as to the security and prosperity of the entire region.

The broad-based support not only has direct benefits for the Ukrainian population but also significantly contributes to the interests of Europe and Germany. A strengthened Ukraine not only offers its own citizens a safe home but also has the potential to thrive economically. It could grow into a significant trading partner for Europe and Germany, which in turn would contribute to strengthening economic relations and general prosperity in the entire region.

Given the existing challenges, it is essential that efforts to support Ukraine are both continuous and intensified. Only through continued and intensified cooperation can sustainable progress in development be achieved and long-term peace in the region be promoted. This urgency underscores the need for a joint commitment by the international community to vigorously support the country on its path to a stable future (BMZ 2024b).

Non-governmental Organisations Spearheading Democracy and Economic Growth

Non-governmental organisations also play a crucial role in promoting democracy, rule of law and human rights in Ukraine. Organisations such as Freedom House and Transparency International monitor compliance with democratic standards, report on human rights violations and support civil society in promoting political participation and transparency. Their commitment helps to strengthen democratic institutions and protect the rights of citizens.

The promotion of economic development and social innovations in Ukraine is of crucial importance in order to put the country on a sustainable economic growth path and improve the living conditions of the population. In this context, non-governmental development actors play a significant role by implementing programmes to promote entrepreneurship, technological innovation and vocational education.

Organisations such as the German Society for International Cooperation (GIZ) and the European Bank for Reconstruction and Development (EBRD) have committed themselves to supporting economic development in Ukraine. Through targeted measures, they contribute to economic growth and social progress (BMZ 2023).

A central approach of these organisations is the promotion of entrepreneurship. By providing training, consulting services and financial support, they help entrepreneurs and founders to implement their business ideas and successfully establish themselves in the market. This not only contributes to the creation of new jobs but also to the diversification of the economy and the strengthening of local communities.

In addition, these organisations focus on technological innovations to increase the competitiveness of the Ukrainian economy. Through investments in research and development and the promotion of high-tech start-ups, they contribute to strengthening the country's innovative power and opening up new growth opportunities.

Another important aspect is the promotion of vocational education. By providing training and further education opportunities, these organisations help to improve the qualifications and skills of the Ukrainian workforce and adapt to the needs of the labour market. This not only contributes to increasing productivity and efficiency but also to combating economic poverty.

The programmes of non-governmental development actors aim to improve the quality of life of the population by facilitating access to education, healthcare, clean water and other basic services. In addition, they promote social innovations and support local communities in addressing social challenges.

It is crucial to continue to support and promote the efforts of non-governmental development actors. This can be done through financial support, technical expertise and political frameworks that create a favourable environment for their activities. Such continuous commitment can contribute to bringing about positive and sustainable change in Ukraine and achieving long-term development goals (especially after the end of the war) (Grävingholt et al. 2023).

Despite their important role, non-governmental development actors in Ukraine face a number of challenges. These include limited resources, political obstacles and security risks. However, they also offer opportunities for positive change and sustainable development. Through partnerships with government agencies, local communities and international organisations, they can amplify their impact and promote long-term solutions to Ukraine's challenges.

Ukraine was already in a phase of profound change before the Russian invasion, characterised by political instability, economic challenges and social upheaval. In this complex context, non-governmental development actors had and continue to have an increasingly significant role in shaping and have taken on the promotion of the country's development process. NGOs, international organisations, foundations and non-profit organisations also presently play a crucial role in the provision of humanitarian aid, the promotion of democracy and human rights, economic development and the introduction of social innovations (BMZ 2024a).

Navigating Challenges, Seizing Opportunities

Particularly in times of political unrest, armed conflicts and natural disasters, non-governmental organisations have played a prominent role in providing humanitarian aid and emergency relief in Ukraine. Organisations such as the Red Cross and Médecins Sans Frontières have proven to be indispensable actors by providing life-saving aid and medical care for injured individuals. Their commitment is crucial in addressing the acute needs of the population in crisis situations and mitigating the impacts of humanitarian disasters.

The Red Cross has implemented a diverse range of humanitarian measures including the provision of medical care for the injured; the distribution of vital relief goods such as food, water and shelter to internally displaced persons; and the support of families affected by the war. Médecins Sans Frontières has also carried out significant humanitarian missions in Ukraine, particularly in areas affected by armed conflicts, where they have provided emergency medical care for injured individuals.

However, the work of these organisations goes beyond the provision of immediate emergency aid. They are also engaged in long-term development projects to strengthen the resilience of communities and support post-war reconstruction. By providing medical care, psychosocial support, educational programmes and income-generating measures, they contribute to laying the foundations for sustainable development and a stable social structure in Ukraine.

The role of non-governmental development actors in the provision of humanitarian aid and emergency relief in Ukraine is crucial and highlights the importance of their work in addressing acute crises and promoting long-term development goals in the region (BMZ 2023).

Guiding Through Complexity: Addressing Ukraine Conflict Challenges

Despite ongoing efforts by Germany and other international actors, the Ukraine conflict remains an extremely complex and persistent challenge of considerable magnitude. The successful implementation of reforms, ensuring humanitarian support and promoting a sustainable peace process continue to be marked by significant difficulties.

Ukraine faces a number of challenges in finding a lasting solution to the conflict and ensuring a stable future. The implementation of reforms, particularly in the area of the rule of law, combating corruption and decentralisation, proves difficult and requires sustained support from the international community. In addition, ensuring humanitarian support for the affected populations remains an urgent necessity, as millions of people continue to suffer from the effects of the conflict.

The future development of the conflict will be significantly influenced by the development of the geopolitical situation in the region, particularly the relations between Ukraine, Russia, the European Union and the United States. Additionally, the internal dynamics of Ukrainian politics and the government's ability to implement reforms and win the support of the population play a crucial role (Meister 2023).

In this context, German development cooperation illustrates Germany's committed advocacy for peace, stability and development in the affected region. Germany contributes to shaping a sustainable future for Ukraine by employing a coordinated and holistic approach. This requires long-term commitment, flexible approaches and close collaboration with local and international partners.

References

Bliman, A. (2024). Ukraine. In W. Gieler & M. Nowak (Eds.), Deutsche Entwicklungszusammenarbeit im Spannungsfeld der Außen- und Sicherheitspolitik. (Re-)konstruktionen – Internationale und Globale Studien (345–379). Wiesbaden.
BMZ. (2023). Entwicklungspolitische Unterstützung der Ukraine. BMZ-Beitrag zum Engagement der Bundesregierung. Retrieved from https://www.bmz.de/resource/blob/108952/entwicklungspolitische-unterstuetzung-der-ukraine.pdf

Bundesministerium für wirtschaftliche Zusammenarbeit und Entwicklung (BMZ). (2024a). Wie arbeitet die deutsche Entwicklungszusammenarbeit? Retrieved from https://www.bmz.de/de/laender/ukraine

Bundesministerium für wirtschaftliche Zusammenarbeit und Entwicklung (BMZ). (2024b, February 22). Entwicklungspolitisches Engagement Deutschlands in der Ukraine [PDF document]. Retrieved from https://www.bmz.de/resource/blob/200710/240222-bmz-engagement-ukraine-stand-22-02-2024.pdf

Bundesregierung. (2024, February 16). Vereinbarung über Sicherheitszusammenarbeit und langfristige Unterstützung zwischen der Bundesrepublik Deutschland und der Ukraine [PDF document]. Retrieved from https://www.bundesregierung.de/resource/blob/2008726/2260264/8efa1868839ede7609437b341d75c3c5/2024-02-16-ukraine-sicherheitsvereinbarung-deu-data.pdf?download=1

Federal Government (2024, February 16).

Grävingholt, J., et al. (2023). Wiederaufbau in der Ukraine: Was die internationale Gemeinschaft jetzt beachten muss. IDOS Policy Brief 2/2023. IDOS, Bonn.

Meister, S. (2023, January 18). Russlands Krieg gegen die Ukraine: Neugestaltung der östlichen EU-Nachbarschaftspolitik. Heinrich-Böll-Stiftung. Retrieved from https://www.boell.de/de/2023/01/18/russlands-krieg-gegen-die-ukraine-neugestaltung-der-oestlichen-eu-nachbarschaftspolitik

OECD. (2023). Bericht über die offizielle Entwicklungszusammenarbeit.

UNHCR. (2022). Bericht über ukrainische Geflüchtete.

Urech, F. (2023, April 13). Wegen rekordhoher Asylkosten und der Ukraine-Hilfe: neuer Höchststand bei den Entwicklungshilfegeldern. NZZ.

Zapf, M., Michel, M., & Leonhard, R. (2023, April 20). Die Ukraine kriegt am meisten. Welt-Sichten: Magazin für globale Entwicklung und ökumenische Zusammenarbeit.

Chapter 7
The Bundeswehr as Actor in the Field of Developmental Policy: A New Perspective on Security and Development

Meik Nowak

Abstract The question of the development policy impact of the Bundeswehr and a consideration of German and international security policy through the lens of development cooperation may still be unusual even after the experiences in Afghanistan. Traditionally, the Bundeswehr is a valued partner in cases of international disaster relief and humanitarian aid; the first international deployment of the Bundeswehr was the logistical support of emergency aid during the earthquake in Agadir in Algeria in 1960. Since then, much has changed, and this article takes a look at the recent history of the Bundeswehr in the field of ICM (international crisis management). In particular, the longest armed deployment in the history of the Bundeswehr in Afghanistan and the White Paper 2016 as a response to the growing security policy tasks are viewed from a development policy perspective.

Development Cooperation and Its Relationship to Security and Defence Policy

This relationship is characterised by the tension between war and peace and a fundamental change in the Bundeswehr on the one side and both massive budget and significance increases on the part of development cooperation (Gieler and Nowak 2021). The peace mission in Afghanistan evolved over time into combat deployment, in which ground troops of the Bundeswehr were involved for the first time and a separation into a civil-peaceful and a military-fighting engagement was no longer viable at a certain point. German soldiers fought, killed, were wounded and fell in combat. Development workers and employees of aid organisations suffered

M. Nowak (✉)
Geistes- und Sozialwissenschaften, Helmut-Schmidt-Universität,
Hamburg, Hamburg, Germany
e-mail: nowakme@hsu-hh.de

© The Author(s), under exclusive license to Springer Fachmedien Wiesbaden GmbH, part of Springer Nature 2024
W. Gieler, M. Nowak (eds.), *Understanding German Development Cooperation*, Contributions to Political Science, https://doi.org/10.1007/978-3-658-45596-5_7

from the steadily deteriorating security situation and were confronted with new challenges.

At the same time, politics and society in Germany struggled for a long time to speak of a war in Afghanistan. In recent years, a convergence of both policy fields has been observed—as well as the realisation that the Bundeswehr as a guarantor of security could create the framework that development policy actors must fill with life (Baxmann 2017; Kappel 2017; Gieler and Nowak 2021).

Thus, already in the 2018 coalition agreement, more funds were allocated for development cooperation, civil crisis prevention, humanitarian aid, defence and the Bundeswehr. These additional financial resources for the areas of "security and defence" as well as "development cooperation" and "humanitarian aid" were increased in a 1:1 ratio (Koalitionsvertrag 2018). With this memorable formula, the coalition agreement of the federal government made up of CDU, SPD and CSU established a correspondence rule between possible financial increases in the defence budget and parts of the budget for development cooperation, which should ensure growing financial resources for the responsible Federal Ministry for Economic Cooperation and Development (BMZ) also in the future.

A driver in the budget was the Ministry of Defence, as with the goal of 2% of gross domestic product for defence spending within the framework of NATO planning, a strong political guideline existed and still exists (BMVg 2018).

Since 2021, there has been a new composition in the Bundestag and thus since September 2021 also a new government. And the traffic light coalition of SPD, Greens and FDP has announced that it wants to do some things differently in the foreign deployments of the Bundeswehr (Koalitionsvertrag 2021). Thus, the traffic light parties agreed in the coalition agreement of December 2021:

> As a reliable partner in systems of collective security we will stick to our foreign and security policy commitment. Nevertheless, every deployment of the Bundeswehr must be preceded by a critical-content confrontation and a review of the prerequisites must precede, as well as the development of possible exit strategies. The use of military force is for us the ultimate means and must always be integrated into a realistic political processing of conflicts and their causes. Armed deployments of the Bundeswehr abroad must be embedded in a system of mutual collective security, based on the Basic Law and international law. We will ensure regular evaluation of ongoing foreign deployments. (Koalitionsvertrag 2021, 150)

For the renewed mandate of foreign deployments, this formulation in the coalition agreement alone will not be significant. The Greens, who were still in opposition in the previous votes, are now not only in government—they also provide the Foreign Minister and thus the head of the Foreign Office, which is primarily responsible for the preparation of the mandates as the basis for foreign deployments of the Bundeswehr. In some of the last decisions on foreign deployments, the Green Party members, often in contrast to the SPD and FDP, voted against or abstained. The question here is how they will behave in the future when it comes to extending the mandate in Mali or even Kosovo. Because the coalition agreement states the following about Germany's future role:

The major challenges of our time can only be met in international cooperation and together in a strong European Union. We are committed to Germany's global responsibility as a major industrial nation in the world. Our commitment to peace, freedom, human rights, democracy, the rule of law and sustainability is an indispensable part of successful and credible foreign policy. We are committed to our humanitarian protection responsibility and want to regulate the procedures for flight and migration. (Koalitionsvertrag 2021, 7)

However, Russia's current attack on Ukraine is changing the view of the relationship between the two policy fields. National and alliance defence has taken on a new significance since 24 February 2022, and the personal equipment and capabilities of the soldiers have taken on a new urgency. The Bundeswehr is being equipped with a special fund of 100 billion euros—something for which there is no civilian development policy counterpart. Against this background, this article also looks back at the question of whether and how the Bundeswehr and development cooperation have changed in recent years and how they have dealt with new and old challenges (Meyer zum Felde 2020; Ferber 2022; Gönner 2022). The war in Ukraine has brought a war on European soil—after the civil war in the disintegrating Yugoslavia of the 1990s of the last century—not only closer in geographical terms but also the constants and coordinates of the previous European peace and security order have been erased.

This is a security policy turnaround that is accompanied by a massive increase in defence spending and the strengthening of NATO in response to Russian aggression (Schröder 2022). This turnaround has development policy implications that are, for example, reflected in the area of food security through declining food exports from Ukraine or in increasing numbers in the area of flight, displacement and migration in neighbouring countries and Europe (Schulze 2022). Another danger is the factor that other conflict hotspots in other parts of the globe such as Yemen and Syria or countries where authoritarian regimes suppress and persecute their own population, such as Myanmar, Afghanistan or Mali, are overlooked or neglected when a conflict is overly focused on. Because war and flight are not only a bitter reality in Ukraine, people are persecuted in many places because of their origin, their faith and their convictions.

Even though it is very easy to attribute the conflicts to the gaping economic gap between the Global North and the Global South and to global injustice, it is still the case—despite China's rise as a global superpower—that societal and economic poverty and wealth are mostly distributed along the lines of North and South (Hareuveni 2014; Rühle 2022). Furthermore, it can be observed that conflicts over scarce resources are increasing in many emerging and developing countries (Rühle 2022; Strack-Zimmermann 2022).

From both a security policy and development policy perspective, therefore, the implementation of the UN Sustainable Development Goals is an important factor. Because peace and justice are indispensable building blocks of sustainable development and the 2030 Agenda, they have to be guaranteed by the respective actors (Hareuveni 2014). Thus, the 2030 Agenda already states in its preamble that without sustainable development there can be no peace and without peace there can be no sustainable development (United Nations 2015).

The Heretical Question of the Development Policy Effects of Security

Since 2015, there has been an increasing demand in specialist discussions and also in the political sphere for an analysis of the actual—i.e. intended and unintended—effects of the Bundeswehr's operations (Dembinski and Gromes 2016). Because many of the previous operations of the Bundeswehr fall into the category of so-called humanitarian military interventions, which—even after Afghanistan and despite the situation in Mali—will constitute a significant part of foreign operations in the foreseeable future, the relationships between military, civil-military and civil perspectives will be a top priority (Bundestag 2015; Kommando Heer 2021). Humanitarian interventions are usually characterised by a state classically sending troops into another state and authorising them to use possible and probable violence with the aim of protecting foreign human lives (Pape 2012).

This does not have to be the sole motive, but it must be recognisable (Tesón 2017). Knowledge about the probabilities of success and conditions for success of these operations is important for advising, analysing and above all designing these operations and their underlying mandates (Zorn 2021, 2022). A general evaluation of the humanitarian military interventions would therefore not only be desirable but also necessary in terms of their legitimacy, their effectiveness in terms of achieving objectives and efficiency in terms of implementation design. However, to date, in the evaluation research of civil-military interventions, it is unclear what the procedures as effects of these operations can methodically reveal beyond a pure output analysis (Fortna 2008; Dembinski and Gromes 2021).

In the development policy discussion about a possible development policy mandate also in the broadest sense of the White Paper 2016 and the concept of the "comprehensive approach", there is often a call for evaluations (Schaper 2015; Baur 2016; AA 2017; Gönner 2022; Schröder 2022). Since 2015, this discussion is no longer purely development-related, as in January 2016 the factions of the CDU/CSU and the SPD presented a draft law to the Bundestag, which provides for the evaluation of foreign operations of the Bundeswehr (Bundestag 2016).

In the following years, little has happened, so that virtually every year debates about the extension of the Bundeswehr's foreign operations begin anew (Meister 2019). As recently as January 2022, the newly elected Bundestag had to decide whether the mandate for the German participation in the anti-IS coalition in Syria and Iraq expiring at the end of the month will be renewed and also the other missions are up for renewal in the following months. 2022 was an interesting year in the consideration of the areas of operation and their development policy implications also because the then largest foreign operation—the Mission Resolute Support in Afghanistan—has now ended. But also the then largest present area of operation in Mali and Niger went into liquidation. Until 2023, the Bundeswehr was active in Mali (and in the context of the Joint Special Operations Task Force Gazelle also in the neighbouring state of Niger). The Bundeswehr's participation in the UN mission MINUSMA and the EU training mission EUTM Mali was due to political instability, Russia's involvement with the private military contractor "Wagner Group" and inter-ethnic clashes subject to political discussion in the German parliament, and despite the difficult situation in the West African countries, German foreign and development policy named Western Africa an important geopolitical region. Nevertheless, the military mandates were not extended in the German parliament, and with the end of the UN and EU Missions due to political pressure of the Malian and Nigerian governments, the operations ended. At the mid of December 2023, the deployment and the last German soldiers left Mali with the formal end of the military assistance in the context of EUTM and MINUSMA. Technically, MINUSMA ended in December 2023, but still the logistic contingent of the Bundeswehr in Niger counts until May 2024 as UN operation as the assets of MINUSMA must be logistically settled and the mission will be closed after this technical liquidation is done.

The Bundeswehr in Action

Presently in 2024, there are ten foreign operations mandated by the Parliament, a UN observer mission without a mandate and seven so-called equivalent commitments. Of the present 18 missions, ten have been provided with a so-called mandate by the Bundestag. This parliamentary reservation is always necessary when involvement in a military conflict is realistic and the use of military force to enforce the mission according to established rules ("rules of engagement") is permitted. For some (observer) missions of the United Nations, a mandate from the Bundestag was requested by the federal government, and for others not. In the international legal view, it is of crucial interest whether it is predominantly about the deployment of armed forces or whether the mission is merely conceived as an observer mission (Bundestag 2015; Rühle 2022).

The deployment of armed forces does not yet imply inherent combat operations, as depending on the mission, participation in combat operations is expressly excluded in the mandate and even the appropriate self-protection in the event of a threat to life and limb is regulated (Ulbert and Werthes 2008). In addition, the so-called recognised missions within NATO territory are relevant, but usually no approval from the Bundestag is required for these. In principle, foreign deployments of German armed forces always take place in a multinational context within the framework of collective security systems; these are usually organisations such as the UN, NATO or the EU.

The exception presently is the international coalition in the fight against the terrorist organisation IS, Operation Inherent Resolve. The Bundeswehr is presently (May 2024) present in a total of ten countries on three continents in different formats and with different forces after the withdrawal from both Afghanistan and Mali and the associated end of the mandates. In addition to clearly defined and geographically named target countries, there are also regional and transnational areas of operation, especially within the framework of maritime forces (such as in the Aegean, the Mediterranean and the Indian Ocean).

In addition, there are another foreign deployments without a mandate within the framework of the UN Mission for the Referendum in Western Sahara (MINURSO) and the equivalent commitments within the framework of the NATO battle group "enhanced Forward Presence" in Lithuania and the surveillance mission Sea Guardian in the Aegean. As part of security policy commitments of varying strength and different time horizons, the Bundeswehr's participation in the permanent maritime task forces of NATO, NATO Air Policing in other member states of the Alliance and the NATO Response Force/Very High Readiness Joint Task Force is also a kind of special foreign deployment but does not follow the understanding of a humanitarian intervention.

Nevertheless, the idea of a comprehensive approach is given in every foreign deployment, and thus a mandate can theoretically arise with respect to the area of operation and the mission (Dicke 2013; Baxmann 2017). An example was the training of special forces of the armed forces of the West African state of Niger without a mandate within the framework of Operation Gazelle and the patrol trip of a German warship to monitor migration flows and smuggling activities in the sea area between the Turkish mainland and the Greek islands of Lesbos and Chios in the wider context of the maritime NATO surveillance mission Sea Guardian, which has been taking place since February 2022.

The Bundeswehr and Its Guiding Principles Over Time

Development cooperation was never an original objective of the soldier's self-understanding (Neitzel 2020). But the four pillars of the soldier's self-understanding are essential to understand the actions and decision-making logics in action. Thus, the legitimacy in the sense of a legal, political and ethical justification of the mandate is as important as integration, in order to define the basic law as a binding framework for soldierly action. Thirdly, the organisationof the mission and its internal logic are important as the design of the internal order for readiness and discipline and ultimately the motivation that duty fulfilment, obedience and discipline arise from the insight of the necessity of the task.

These four aspects are important for understanding mandates, recognising the meaningfulness of soldierly action and therefore timely for the resilience of soldiers and the concept of a lived error culture. These four points provide a clue as to why the Bundeswehr often retreats to the safe ground of a mandate and usually views the complex development policy world with intended and unintended goals sceptically. Finally the self-image of soldiers is to be located between tradition and contradiction—and if there is no civil-military tradition in Germany or merely an instrumental role of the Bundeswehr as a security service provider or global logistician, then soldiers cannot live this role either (Buchner 2022; Dörfer-Dierken 2022).

Ultimately, the deployment, which can include war, is a political act, and the soldiers need the rhythm of judgement or the verdict of the public, which reflects the meaningfulness of their actions. This was not the case in Afghanistan, and whether it is different in Mali remains to be seen. The profession of a soldier is a political profession (Meister 2019). A soldier has a political mandate, which must be translated into the military and at the same time translated back into the political. The concept of soldiers as citizens in uniform is therefore perhaps dusty but still powerful (Neitzel 2020; Buchner 2022).

With regard to the internal structure of the Bundeswehr and the confrontation with peace, security and development, there is still a connection between militancy and masculinity in an association chain of military—fighting—war. This also has something to do with the fact that, in the Bundeswehr, socialisation takes place through a homosocial group identity in the comradeship prescribed in § 12 and the key symbol of the soldier as a fighter in service for Germany—and not as a service provider or development aid worker. One possible reason for this association chain is certainly the fact that, in the Bundeswehr, women, voters of the Greens and the Left Party as well as people from the milieu of performers, expeditives and hedonists are underrepresented (Neitzel 2020; Buchner 2022).

But one must also see how long the development path of the Bundeswehr is, so it may not be surprising if the Bundeswehr does not see itself as a development policy actor. In 1955, the Bundeswehr was founded in the Cold War, and then in 1956 conscription was introduced, and horror stories about the Bund, old war veterans, old Wehrmacht and Waffen-SS comrades in leadership positions, neo-Nazi activities, drill and a veritable cornucopia of Bundeswehr scandals in an age between security policy deterrence and a beginning dialogue made the rounds. Nuclear war was a possible, realistic danger, and the fear of it reached its peak in the 1980s with a strengthened peace movement in a numerically huge Bundeswehr and nuclear armament.

With reunification and the self-designation as the "Army of Unity" as well as the integration of the former NVA into the Bundeswehr with simultaneous massive reduction of personnel, alliance and national defence was also imprinted into the self-understanding of the soldiers in the 1990s despite military engagement in the Western Balkans (Neitzel 2020). Only in the wake of the attacks of 11 September 2001 and the engagement in Afghanistan did the Bundeswehr become an army in worldwide deployment, in which women could also become soldiers in all career groups. Only through the numerically increasing and longer-lasting deployments in Bosnia, Kosovo and Afghanistan did the soldiers came into contact with development policy actors beyond disaster relief missions in case of natural disasters or relatively small UN missions (Oswald and Toetzke 2015; Rücker 2015; Schmidt 2015). Only the creation of a professional army between international crisis management, interventions and alliance defence after the suspension of conscription and a functional specialisation after several transformations (BMVg 2013) has actually created military guiding, professional and self-images in relation to development policy issues, in the areas of operation but also after the operation at home in Germany (Neitzel 2020).

Fundamentally, the goal of military action is the establishment or securing of peace under the threat and use of violence (Neitzel 2020; Dörfer-Dierken 2022). The use of violence is understood from this perspective as a means to achieve peaceful purposes, not as a goal or end in itself of military action. Until 1989/1990, national defence was the focus of the professional images, but since the 1990s, so-called peace-creating and peace-securing operations in internal or cross-border conflicts have been shaping the self-image of soldiers as "new", additional tasks. Militarily, the self-image fluctuates in the classic inter-state wars between the fighter and inspiring troop leader, the type of manager and technician, to the diplomatically, politically and academically educated soldier in the highly complex operational scenarios of the present and soldiers as diplomats, helpers, protectors or even social workers (Neitzel 2020; Vollmer 2022).

Security Without Development?

In the question of the success or failure of military action, it is obvious to use the evaluations of the individual German deployment contingents in an evaluation of the military deployment (Dembinski and Gromes 2021). However, this should not only be limited to the short-term and rapid drawing of necessary military conclusions for operational leadership, training and the use of necessary equipment. Here, the question of learning effects and the consideration of higher-level aspects for subsequent contingents in the area of operation in the sense of task-related learning or routine action to be transferred learning, which is reflected in the operational principles of the Bundeswehr, becomes very clear. The personal equipment of the soldiers and their operation-related training are based on the experiences gained in Afghanistan.

The question of the totality of all effects of the military deployment on the situation in Afghanistan is more than just increasing one's own learning capacity. Especially in the area of civil-military cooperation, it would be helpful to fall back on patterns and approaches of development cooperation or to exchange with the acting persons also in this field (Schaper 2015). Thus, development cooperation has the *peace and conflict assessment (PCA)* instead of the rules of engagement (RoE) as a similar guideline, at least as far as project implementation is concerned. The state actors GIZ and KfW are obliged to carry out a PCA for programme proposals in fragile contexts and to present this in the programme proposals to the country departments. The BMZ sector department "Peace and Security, Disaster Risk Management" then monitors compliance with these minimum standards (BMZ 2013, 2020a).

Successful civil-military cooperation is therefore based on the successful, inclusive and ideally participatory access of the population in the area of operation to the state's security services (Oswald and Toetzke 2015; Schaper 2015). These are embedded in a network of trust relationships between citizens and the state with its institutions. A corresponding strengthening of regional security cooperation can be achieved by the so-called local ownership for national SSR processes, which allows for successful "capacity-building" in the sense of self-help and constructive state-society relationships. Classic instruments include disarmament, demobilisation and reintegration (*DDR: disarmament, demobilisation and reintegration*), a joint peace-educational work on the past and reconciliation justice in the sense of transitional justice, the control of (small) arms and prevention of the recruitment of child soldiers, as well as partner-oriented advice on national reforms and security strategies. Ideally, all these instruments require a cross-departmental German foreign and security policy (Waldenhof 2019; Meyer zum Felde 2020).

The Bundeswehr operates according to its self-image and the ministerial guidelines in foreign missions as an instrument of German security policy. Thus, the Bundeswehr does not pursue its own approach in development cooperation. A minimum level of security, which is also promoted by Bundeswehr missions, is a prerequisite for the work of humanitarian aid organisations and successful development cooperation. German and international development cooperation can be supported by the Bundeswehr, if it promotes the implementation of military activities, within the scope of available capacities and/or in the context of humanitarian emergency and disaster relief. Moreover, the Bundeswehr has not shown any ambitions to create a development policy mandate on its own—ultimately, this is not its task.

Most examples of successful civil-military cooperation between civilian and military actors have taken place particularly in the context of humanitarian emergency and disaster relief (Klingebiel and Roehder 2004; BMVg 2018; Zorn 2022).

The claim of the Bundeswehr and the ministerial department is however much stronger, as the aspects of a stronger interlocking are set out in the White Paper 2016 under the slogan "Sustainably shaping security":

> The sustainable safeguarding of security interests is a generational responsibility. Sustainable security means, equally linking the security of states, people and subsequent generations as well as the diverse connections between development and security. With the already initiated reversal of trend in the prospective resource allocation, – with appropriate consolidation – German foreign, security, defence and development policy can meet the known and expected challenges. A flexible and sustainable orientation ensures the rapid response also to difficult to foresee events and emerging threats. Only in this way can the necessary protection of people in Germany be planned and shaped. (BMVg 2016, p. 40)

The other two major intersections include the concept of "human security" as well as the Bundeswehr's and the BMVg's commitment to the 2030 Agenda and the global sustainability goals:

> With the Agenda 2030 for sustainable development, the world community in 2015 for the first time explicitly recognised the inseparable connection between peace and security with sustainable development and the validity of human rights. Peace and security are created permanently only in and between constitutional and inclusive societies with good governance and efficient institutions. A partnership-based world order, the fair design of globalisation, the commitment to the universal validity of human rights, the fight against extreme poverty and hunger and the protection of our natural livelihoods, so that all people in their homeland have the chance of a life in dignity, the creation of human security worldwide – all this contributes to our national security. (BMVg 2016, 62)

But also in the context of arms control and peacekeeping, the military actors within the framework of the White Paper pursue a rather classic development policy approach of partner orientation and multilateral cooperation:

> Germany will advocate even more emphatically for comprehensive agreements on military confidence-building, limiting destabilising military developments, and consistently preventing the proliferation of weapons of mass destruction within a regional and global framework. In this, we rely on a multilateral and cooperative approach. (BMVg 2016, 82)

Institutional Intersections of the Subject Areas

The role of the BAKS is of particular interest for the institutional interlinking of the two subject and policy areas. The Federal Academy for Security Policy was founded in 1992 as a cross-departmental internal training and further education institution of the Federal Republic of Germany in the field of security policy and is subordinate to the Federal Security Council. Same is for the relationship of security policy actors in the area of the Bundeswehr to the BMZ and AA in the sense of the comprehensive approach and civil-military interactions. In response to the changing geopolitical situation, a stronger interlinking with regional and development policy contexts was pursued at the beginning of the millennium (Klingebiel and Roehder 2004).

As part of strategic early detection and foresight, the respective department-bound crisis early warning instruments of both the AA and the BMVg as well as the BMZ have been adapted and more closely interlinked since 2018 (BMVg 2018; BMZ 2020b). This process of joint strategic early detection of crises is not yet complete, but through joint working groups and the mirroring or exchange of posts between the ministries, a harmonisation and bundling of competencies is envisaged. Nonetheless, each of the three ministries has its own IT-supported instrument—the Foreign Office uses PREVIEW (prediction, visualisation, early warning), the BMVg the IT supported forecasting tools and analysis predictions in their crisis early detection within the framework of the pilot project "Competence Centre for Crisis Early Detection" of the University of the Bundeswehr in Munich and the BMZ produces an annual country-specific qualitative escalation potential analysis, which is supplemented by the annual escalation potential analysis commissioned by the Leibniz Institute for Global and Regional Studies (BMVg 2018; BMZ 2020a, b).

Other initiatives include the bundling of peace and conflict research expertise and an exchange of academic and practical knowledge in discussion forums and platforms such as the "PeaceLab" (König 2019). But this beginning interlinking of expertise is lived out, for example, through the network "Strategic Foresight in Practice", which the BAKS organises annually and brought together content partners such as the Federal Ministry for Economic Cooperation and Development (BMZ) in 2019 on the topic of "The Africa of the Future" with security policy practitioners. Just like the Common Effort Community of the First German-Dutch Corps (1GNC)—which has existed since 2010—this is a method to break out of old thought patterns and to practice practical exercises and exchange formats for civil-military cooperation together with civilian experts, diplomats and development workers (Halbauer 2015; Gönner 2022).

Another format of inter-ministerial cooperation is the EZ-College of the BMZ, which among other things is intended to stimulate thinking about development and security together. Since the illegitimate exercise of violence and corresponding weak state structures are disadvantageous and make broad-based and sustainable development more difficult, the connection between security and development is evident, and the relationship can be described with a nexus between security and development, but questions about determining factors of comprehensive action and relevant actors in the respective target countries can only be solved together (Oswald and Toetzke 2015; Halbauer 2015; BMZ 2020a; Schröder 2022).

As soon as development policy is understood as a response to global future tasks, an understanding based on a comprehensive approach to policy fields is usually within reach. This understanding can be supplemented by the expansion of the relationship between security and development, as development policy is always also peace policy. This is all the more so as there are also desires in international cooperation regarding equipment, empowerment and training by German soldiers (Fuhrmann et al. 2017).

Since 2017, the BAKS has been advocating for stronger integration of development policy perspectives into the security policy discussion and for achieving an understanding among decision-makers that a minimum level of security is a basic prerequisite for sustainable development. Because sustainable development requires a dialogue and a partnership-based, trustful cooperation with the responsible actors on site, the number of practices and successfull joint activities is limited to certain partner countries. Uncertainty between state actors committed to a goal can result in inaccessibility of partners and action spaces and thus inhibit development potential at all levels.

In summary, anyone who is active in developing countries of the Global South also has a role in development policy. Even if it is by providing security and training security actors as part of a security agenda. Because the GIZ also works with the Federal Ministry of Defence in the field of German international cooperation, there are examples of civil-military activities and initiatives touching both security and developmental issues. Since June 2011, there has been a cooperation agreement which regulates and institutionalises the cooperation between the Bundeswehr and the GIZ in peace-building and stabilising measures in partner countries. This partnership was deepened in 2014 through a cooperation between the GIZ and the Bundeswehr Command Academy.

In the past, the GIZ was mostly commissioned with the planning and execution of construction measures within the framework of international peace missions, such as in Kosovo and Afghanistan. But for some years now, this rather technical solution has been moving further into the background and the substantive expertise or implementation of projects of civil-military cooperation. Since 2016, the GIZ has been commissioned from the newly created budget title "Empowerment of partner states in the field of security, defence and stabilisation", which is jointly managed by the Foreign Office and the BMVg, particularly in Africa.

To solve the problem of different mandates of development cooperation and security policy actors, it is necessary to identify basic conditions and to consolidate them (Bartels & Glatz 2018; Dembinski and Gromes 2021; Zorn 2022). These are as follows:

- Clearly defined mandates for civilian and military actors.
- Clear communication and coordination.
- Context-specific guidelines at strategic, tactical and operational level.

The core question of whether peace is militarily enforced and remains civil cannot be answered unequivocally. The basic issue, however, is made clear in the rather old but still present text by Siegmar Schmidt:

> The demand of the Federal President Joachim Gauck in January 2014, that Germany should take on more responsibility in the world, which is also expressly supported by the federal government, could tend to strengthen development cooperation as part of security policy. To what extent the security policy orientation of development cooperation increases or rather decreases the acceptance of development policy and foreign policy must currently remain open. (Schmidt 2015, 35)

References

AA – Auswärtiges Amt (Hrsg.). (2017). *Krisen verhindern, Konflikte bewältigen, Frieden fördern. Leitlinien der Bundesregierung.* Berlin
Bartels, H.-P. & Glatz, R. (2018). *Welche Reform die Bundeswehr heute braucht – Ein Denkanstoß.* SWP-Aktuell 2020/A 84. Berlin.
Baur, H.-P. (2016). Vernetzte Entwicklung: Gemeinsames Ziel guter Entwicklungs-, Sicherheits- und Außenpolitik. In: Wagner, R. & Schaprian, H.-J. (Hrsg.): *Komplexe Krisen – aktive Verantwortung. Magdeburger Gespräche zur Friedens- und Sicherheitspolitik.* 75–79. Magdeburg.
Baxmann, M. (2017). Hilfreiches Prinzipienreiten: Wie die Agenda 2030 friedlichen Wandel in Konfliktsituationen ermöglichen kann. *FriEnt Briefing Nr. 12*, Bonn.
BMVg – Bundesministerium der Verteidigung (Hrsg.) (2013). *Die Neuausrichtung der Bundeswehr. Nationale Interessen wahren – Internationale Verantwortung übernehmen – Sicherheit gemeinsam gestalten.* Berlin.
BMVg – Bundesministerium der Verteidigung (Hrsg.) (2016). *Weissbuch 2016 zur Sicherheitspolitik Deutschlands und zur Zukunft der Bundeswehr.* Berlin.
BMVg – Bundesministerium der Verteidigung (Hrsg.) (2018). *Konzeption der Bundeswehr.* Berlin.
BMZ – Bundesministerium für wirtschaftliche Zusammenarbeit und Entwicklung (Hrsg.) (2013). *Entwicklung für Frieden und Sicherheit. Entwicklungspolitisches Engagement im Kontext von Konflikt, Fragilität und Gewalt.* BMZ-Strategiepapier 4/2013
BMZ – Bundesministerium für wirtschaftliche Zusammenarbeit und Entwicklung (Hrsg.) (2020a). *Erfahrungen aus der Praxis des Humanitarian-Development-Peace Nexus – eine Literatursichtung.* Bonn und Berlin.
BMZ – Bundesministerium für wirtschaftliche Zusammenarbeit und Entwicklung (Hrsg.) (2020b). *Strategie der strukturbildenden Übergangshilfe. Krisen bewältigen, Resilienz stärken, Perspektiven schaffen.* Bonn und Berlin.

Buchner, P. (2022). Gesangverein oder Kontemplation? Zur Parlamentarmee Bundeswehr. In: Elbe, M. (Hrsg.). *Philosophie des Militärs*. Wiesbaden. 131–152.
Bundestag (2015). *Abschlussbericht der Kommission zur Überprüfung und Sicherung der Parlamentsrechte bei der Mandatierung von Auslandseinsätzen der Bundeswehr*. Bundestags-Drucksache 18/5000. Berlin.
Bundestag (2016). *Entwurf eines Gesetzes zur Fortentwicklung der parlamentarischen Beteiligung bei der Entscheidung über den Einsatz bewaffneter Streitkräfte im Ausland im Zuge fortschreitender Bündnisintegration*. Bundestags-Drucksache 18/7360. Berlin.
Dembinski, M. & Gromes, T. (2016). Auslandseinsätze evaluieren. Wie lässt sich Orientierungswissen zu humanitären Interventionen gewinnen? *HSFK-Report Nr. 8/2016*. Frankfurt am Main.
Dembinski, M. & Gromes, T. (2021). Afghanistan aufarbeiten. Den Einsatz nachträglich legitimieren oder Entscheidungshilfen für die Zukunft liefern? *PRIF Spotlight 14/2021*. Frankfurt am Main.
Dicke, V. (2013). Vergessene Prinzipien, In: *E+Z, Jg. 54, Nr. 11*, 430–432.
Dörfer-Dierken, A. (2022). Si vis pacem … – Gerechter Krieg oder gerechter Frieden? In: Elbe, M. (Hrsg.). *Philosophie des Militärs*. Wiesbaden. 201–230.
Ferber, M. (2022). Frieden durch nachhaltige Sicherheit – Was die EU jetzt tun muss. In: Behörden Spiegel-Gruppe in Zusammenarbeit mit dem Bundesverband der Deutschen Sicherheits- und Verteidigungsindustrie e.V. (BDSV) (Hrsg.): *Frieden, Sicherheit, Nachhaltigkeit – Beiträge zu einer gesellschaftspolitischen Debatte*. Bonn. 10–11.
Fortna, V. (2008). *Does Peacekeeping Work? Shaping Belligerents' Choices after Civil War*. Princeton.
Fuhrmann, J.; Herlitze, A.-K.; Strauß, L.; Walravens, H. (2017). Ertüchtigung regionaler Partner: Vier Anforderungen an ein "neues" Instrument der Krisenprävention. *BAKS-Arbeitspapier 27/2019*. Berlin.
Gieler, W. & Nowak, M. (Hrsg.) (2021). *Staatliche Entwicklungszusammenarbeit in Deutschland: Eine Bestandsaufnahme des BMZ 1961–2021*. Wiesbaden.
Gönner, T. (2022). Sicherheit durch Nachhaltigkeit – Vernetzt arbeiten für eine krisenfestere Welt. In: Behörden Spiegel-Gruppe in Zusammenarbeit mit dem Bundesverband der Deutschen Sicherheits- und Verteidigungsindustrie e.V. (BDSV) (Hrsg.): *Frieden, Sicherheit, Nachhaltigkeit – Beiträge zu einer gesellschaftspolitischen Debatte*. Bonn. 30–31.
Halbauer, V. (2015). Der Comprehensive Approach – Teil der „Gene" des I. (Deutsch/Niederländischen) Korps. In: Schröder, R. & Hansen, S. (2015). *Stabilisierungseinsätze als gesamtstaatliche Aufgabe – Erfahrungen und Lehren aus dem deutschen Afghanistaneinsatz zwischen Staatsaufbau und Aufstandsbewältigung (COIN)*. Baden-Baden. 103–116.
Hareuveni, E. (2014). *The Lawless Zone. The Transfer of Policing and Security powers to the civilian security coordinators in the settlements and outposts*. Tel Aviv.
Kommando Heer (Hrsg.) (2021). *Operative Leitlinien des Heeres zur Zukunft deutscher Landstreitkräfte 2030+*. Strausberg.
Kappel, R. (2017). Deutschlands Rolle als Zivilmacht. In: Ischinger, W. & Messner, D.: *Deutschlands Neue Verantwortung: Die Zukunft der deutschen und europäischen Außen-, Entwicklungs- und Sicherheitspolitik*. Berlin.
Klingebiel, S., & Roehder, K. (2004). *Militär und Entwicklungspolitik in Post-Konflikt-Situationen*. (AIPA – Arbeitspapiere zur Internationalen Politik und Außenpolitik, 4/2004). Köln.
Koalitionsvertrag 2021–2025 zwischen der Sozialdemokratischen Partei Deutschlands (SPD), BÜNDNIS 90 / DIE GRÜNEN und den Freien Demokraten (FDP) (2021). *Mehr Fortschritt wagen – Bündnis für Freiheit, Gerechtigkeit und Nachhaltigkeit*. Berlin.
Koalitionsvertrag zwischen CDU, CSU und SPD (2018). *Ein neuer Aufbruch für Europa. Eine neue Dynamik für Deutschland. Ein neuer Zusammenhalt für unser Land*. Berlin.
König, R. (2019). Peacelab – Zeit für eine Zwischenbilanz. In: *ZUR SACHE BW, Ausgabe 35 1/2019*. 44–46.
Meister, G. (2019). Klempner des Friedens. In: *ZUR SACHE BW, Ausgabe 35 1/2019*. 8–12.

Meyer zum Felde, R. (2020). Deutsche Verteidigungspolitik – Versäumnisse und nicht eingehaltene Versprechen. In: *SIRIUS – Zeitschrift für Strategische Analysen, 4 (3)*. 315–332.
Neitzel, S. (2020). *Deutsche Krieger. Vom Kaiserreich zur Berliner Republik – eine Militärgeschichte*. Berlin.
Oswald, S. & Toetzke, C. (2015). „Counterinsurgency" (COIN) – Eine entwicklungspolitische Perspektive. In: Schröder, R. & Hansen, S. (2015). *Stabilisierungseinsätze als gesamtstaatliche Aufgabe – Erfahrungen und Lehren aus dem deutschen Afghanistaneinsatz zwischen Staatsaufbau und Aufstandsbewältigung (COIN)*. Baden-Baden. 189–196.
Pape, R (2012). When Duty Calls. A Pragmatic Standard of Humanitarian Intervention, in: *International Security, 37: 1*, 41–80.
Rücker, H. (2015). Die Rolle der Zivilbevölkerung in heutigen Konflikten und die spezifische Bedeutung von CIMIC in Stabilisierungseinsätzen und COIN. In: Schröder, R. & Hansen, S. (2015). *Stabilisierungseinsätze als gesamtstaatliche Aufgabe – Erfahrungen und Lehren aus dem deutschen Afghanistaneinsatz zwischen Staatsaufbau und Aufstandsbewältigung (COIN)*. Baden-Baden. 117–126.
Rühle, M. (2022). Zwischen militärischen Notwendigkeiten und politischen Erwartungen: NATO, Klimawandel und Nachhaltigkeit. In: Behörden Spiegel-Gruppe in Zusammenarbeit mit dem Bundesverband der Deutschen Sicherheits- und Verteidigungsindustrie e.V. (BDSV) (Hrsg.): *Frieden, Sicherheit, Nachhaltigkeit – Beiträge zu einer gesellschaftspolitischen Debatte*. Bonn. 22–25.
Schaper, M. (2015). Konfliktbearbeitung, Stabilisierung und Strategiebildung unter Einbeziehung der Zivilgesellschaft: Warum vernetztes Handeln dringend eine friedenspolitische Leitbilddebatte benötigt. In: Schröder, R. & Hansen, S. (2015). *Stabilisierungseinsätze als gesamtstaatliche Aufgabe – Erfahrungen und Lehren aus dem deutschen Afghanistaneinsatz zwischen Staatsaufbau und Aufstandsbewältigung (COIN)*. Baden-Baden. 91–102.
Schmidt, S. (2015). Entwicklungszusammenarbeit als strategisches Feld deutscher Außenpolitik, in: *Aus Politik und Zeitgeschichte APuZ, (7–9)*, 29–35.
Schröder, U. (2022). Integrierte und umfassende Sicherheitspolitik – Deutschlands Beitrag zu einer nachhaltigen und inklusiven Friedensordnung im 21. Jahrhundert. In: Wagner, R. & Schaprian, H.-J. (Hrsg.): *Zeitenwende in der Sicherheitspolitik – Deutschlands Weg in eine neue Ordnung*, 91–98.
Schulze, S. (2022). Sicherheit erfordert eine starke Entwicklungspolitik. In: Wagner, R. & Schaprian, H.-J. (Hrsg.): *Zeitenwende in der Sicherheitspolitik – Deutschlands Weg in eine neue Ordnung*, 51–60.
Strack-Zimmermann, M.-A. (2022). Die Folgen des Klimawandels bedrohen die weltweite Sicherheit. In: Behörden Spiegel-Gruppe in Zusammenarbeit mit dem Bundesverband der Deutschen Sicherheits- und Verteidigungsindustrie e.V. (BDSV) (Hrsg.): *Frieden, Sicherheit, Nachhaltigkeit – Beiträge zu einer gesellschaftspolitischen Debatte*. Bonn. 15–17.
Tesón, F (2017). A Defense of Humanitarian Intervention, in: Teson, F. & Van der Vossen, B.: *Debating Humanitarian Intervention. Should We Try to Save Strangers?* .New York, 23–150.
Ulbert, C. & Werthes, S. (Hrsg.) (2008). *Menschliche Sicherheit – Globale Herausforderung und regionale Perspektiven*. Baden-Baden.
United Nations. (2015). *Transforming Our World: The 2030 Agenda for Sustainable Development*. New York.
Vollmer, J. (2022). Ohne Frieden wird es keine nachhaltige Entwicklung geben. In: Behörden Spiegel-Gruppe in Zusammenarbeit mit dem Bundesverband der Deutschen Sicherheits- und Verteidigungsindustrie e.V. (BDSV) (Hrsg.): *Frieden, Sicherheit, Nachhaltigkeit – Beiträge zu einer gesellschaftspolitischen Debatte*. Bonn. 20–21.
Waldenhof, B. (2019). Entwicklungspolitik in Zeiten globaler Zukunftsziele, internationaler Machtverschiebungen und vernetzter Außen-, Entwicklungs- und Sicherheitspolitik. In: Sangmeister, H. & Wagner, H.: *Die Entwicklungszusammenarbeit der Zukunft*. Baden-Baden. 185–201
Zorn, E. (2021). Erfolgreiche Auslandseinsätze brauchen den Einsatz aller Mittel. Rede des Generalinspekteurs der Bundeswehr anlässlich der Auftaktveranstaltung „20 Jahre

Afghanistan – Startschuss für eine Bilanzdebatte" am 6. Oktober 2021 in Berlin. https://www.bmvg.de/de/aktuelles/generalinspekteur-afghanistan-einsatz-differenziert-betrachten-5227428

Zorn, E. (2022). Zeitenwende für die Bundeswehr. In: Behörden Spiegel-Gruppe in Zusammenarbeit mit dem Bundesverband der Deutschen Sicherheits- und Verteidigungsindustrie e.V. (BDSV) (Hrsg.): *Frieden, Sicherheit, Nachhaltigkeit – Beiträge zu einer gesellschaftspolitischen Debatte*. Bonn. 18–19.

Chapter 8
Visions and Strategies: The Future of German Government Development Cooperation

Meik Nowak

Abstract At the centre of the discussion is the so-called Zeitenwende of 2022 as a response to Russia's war of aggression against Ukraine. The effects of the "Zeitenwende" on the design of strategies and implications of German development policy are highlighted. Furthermore, the implementation of the development policy "design year" 2015 and the present development policy discussion are analysed. In particular, the resulting challenges and opportunities that arise at the actor level within the framework of German government development cooperation are discussed. Based on nine trend indicators, interfaces and theses for the perspectives of future German government development cooperation are formulated.

"Zeitenwende": A Turning Point—Also in the Field of Development Policy?

An important question in the context of presenting possible perspectives of German government development cooperation, which needs to be answered, is certainly the one about the level of ambition of the actors of government development cooperation. Even after the turning point in 2022, it can be unequivocally stated that the genuine policy field "development cooperation" has gained political relevance, but at the same time the fundamental theoretical vagueness of the concept of development and open points of contention in the social science discourse landscape have been echoing since the 1970s until today (Thiel 2001; Hartmann 2012).

The interfaces to the subject areas "international cooperation" from the perspective of international relations, to "international economic relations" from the perspective of economics (especially macroeconomics), to "international social

M. Nowak (✉)
Geistes- und Sozialwissenschaften, Helmut-Schmidt-Universität, Hamburg, Hamburg, Germany
e-mail: nowakme@hsu-hh.de

© The Author(s), under exclusive license to Springer Fachmedien Wiesbaden GmbH, part of Springer Nature 2024
W. Gieler, M. Nowak (eds.), *Understanding German Development Cooperation*, Contributions to Political Science, https://doi.org/10.1007/978-3-658-45596-5_8

movements" from the perspective of political sociology and to the individual sectoral—mostly regional scientific—approaches such as neighbouring academic disciplines like ethnology or cultural studies also still hold a high academic discourse potential today (Wieczorek-Zeul 2017, Gönner 2022). Also, the question about the role of development cooperation in the context of security policy—unlike peace policy—as an early warning instrument is a strongly discussed topic in German development cooperation in the aftermath of the end of German engagement in Afghanistan and the Russian war of aggression against Ukraine (Schneider et al. 2022; Grävingholt et al. 2023; Wege 2023; Bunde et al. 2024; Leininger and Hornidge 2024).

The following explanations are dedicated to possible scenarios of the (further) development of German government development cooperation. But before we get to the central thesis of the article, three important and present basic documents of German government development cooperation should be briefly introduced and outlined. Compared to other federal ministries and policy fields, development cooperation—and thus the BMZ—is very transparent and open when it comes to strategic orientation. While some voices may still attest a strategy deficit to the BMZ, at least on the output side, there are clear strategy papers existing. Whether these are actually concrete in the project reality and are also accepted and adapted by the individual actors of government development cooperation is left open here for now.

It should be noted that the Agenda 2030 and the 17 SDGs derived from it provide the large global framework for the constitution of German government development cooperation. In the organisational appropriation of the goals for sustainable development, it appears necessary to consider the following central and presently shaping basic documents of German government development cooperation: The decisive documents from the BMZ are certainly the Future Charter (BMZ 2015), the concept for the implementation of the Agenda 2030 as a future contract in the development policy arena (BMZ 2017) and the Reform Concept 2030 (BMZ 2020b). Here, the significance of the policy field is outlined in the face of new challenges:

> Today, more than ever, development policy is expected to deliver. It must provide answers to future questions and the major challenges facing humanity: climate change and environmental destruction, crises and conflicts, flight and migration, securing the basic needs of a steadily growing world population. (BMZ 2020a; 8)

State development cooperation is more in demand than ever in the context of the ever-changing globalised world, to provide new answers to the major challenges (Klingebiel 2020). The aspect of the "Zeitenwende" in 2022 also strongly shapes the design of German development cooperation in the subsequent period—something that also affects the importance of German development cooperation with Ukraine and the allocation of funds to the BMZ in the foreign and security policy strategic target corridor of Germany (Bunde et al. 2024; Leininger and Hornidge 2024).

And these soft challenges of the "flip side of globalisation" are characterised by rising social inequalities, man-made environmental destruction and precarious working conditions along the supply chains of the "Global South", and the hard challenges are in the form of an increasing number of wars, strong growth of the world population, increasing resource consumption, loss of biodiversity and anthropogenic climate change.

The BMZ's Future Charter states:

> In the 21st century, development policy no longer takes place only in distant countries. Because of globalisation, for example through long supply chains, people's living conditions are now intricately linked worldwide. Many raw materials for our mobile phones and computers come from Africa, our clothes from Asia and the soybeans for our livestock feed from fields in South America. These examples show that everyday things like food, clothing or mobile phones no longer work without global connections. This creates a significant number of jobs in developing and emerging countries, but it also means that it increasingly concerns us under what conditions our food, our clothing, our car and our mobile phone are produced worldwide. (BMZ 2015, 7)

The corresponding appeal in the public arena is both societal- and policy-related, that a rethink and reorientation in individual consumer behaviour as well as in societal and/or political action must be seen (Müller 2020). In the positive reading of this political discourse, development policy—and thus also the state development cooperation of the future—can be understood as a cross-cutting task of all national politics in accordance with the Agenda 2030 and the Paris Climate Agreement. In the negative reading, development policy—and thus also the state development cooperation of the future—degenerates into a pseudo-humanitarian fig leaf for a largely strategy-free, vision-free foreign policy with short-term, usually foreign economic motives.

The reality of state development cooperation will lie between these two extreme poles. In the following, without claiming to be exhaustive, nine trend indicators are named which, in my opinion, could play a decisive role in the future design of state German development cooperation.

Nine Trend Indicators of State German Development Cooperation

The **first indicator** for the future design of German state development cooperation is certainly the role of international conferences as an expression of a global governance structure and the derived resolutions of these conferences in the reality of the implementation of development policy guidelines. Here it is necessary to differentiate between a pure multilateral symbolic policy without underpinning by concrete projects and implementations of these projects and a critical appreciation of this international regulatory structure as a framework and conceptual guideline for development cooperation.

After the political optimism of the major development conferences of the 1990s (Bohnet 2015; Stockmann et al. 2016) and the long road to the major conferences in 2015, it is time, 5 years after Paris, Addis Ababa and New York, to consider the creative claim and the development policy reality. Thus, little is felt of the once contemplated reorientation of the BMZ after the "design year 2015" (Klingebiel 2017; Martens and Obenland 2017) in the aftermath of the third international conference on development financing in Addis Ababa on 15 July 2015, the adoption of the Agenda 2030 and the goals for sustainable development (SDGs) by the UN General Assembly within the framework of the World Summit for Sustainable Development in New York from 25 to 27 September 2015 and the final climate conference in Paris (COP 21) from 30 November to 12 December 2015. Although the global sustainability goals act like a bracket of ministerial action on the part of the BMZ, but of a close interlocking of the policy areas including the downstream implementation organisation across the boundaries of the individual specialist departments or even between the federal government and the level of the federal states, despite various good examples, even more activities can take place (Kerkow 2017; Martens and Obenland 2017; Martens and Ellmers 2020).

However, since the 1990s and increasingly since the beginning of Müller's term of office in 2013, the BMZ has made some exceptions at the level of municipalities in the form of strengthening local sustainability initiatives through the SKEW (Service Agency Communities in One World) with increased acceptance of development policy issues by local actors and interest groups (Kerkow 2017; Martens and Obenland 2017). Regardless of the instrument of the major international conferences or the glocalisation of development policy initiatives at city or municipal level, the future poses the creative question of the degree of multilateralism of German state development cooperation (Martens and Scherer 2021).

Here is the role of the present Minister Schulze—who in her previous political career was Federal Minister for Environment, Nature Conservation and Nuclear Safety of the Federal Republic of Germany. The importance of international environmental and climate policy as part of development policy has increased in recent years. An indicator of this is the person of the permanent state secretary in the BMZ. Jochen Flasbarth was from 2013 to 2021 permanent state secretary in the Federal Ministry for Environment, Nature Conservation and Nuclear Safety and from 2009 to 2013 President of the Federal Environment Agency and is considered a distinguished climate expert. He was negotiator of the German delegation 2015 at the climate negotiations of Paris. The BMZ is furthermore very much technically involved in climate financing and the accompaniment of the World Climate Conferences. This strongly characterises the term of office of the present minister despite other crises. In addition, the aid measures and promotions for Ukraine—although usually media-covered by the Foreign Office or the Federal Ministry of Defence—as well as the coordination of the reconstruction of Ukraine are located in the organisation and implementation processes of the BMZ (Grävingholt et al. 2023).

The **second indicator** is also historically located in the years 2015 and 2016 and can only be inadequately characterised with the catchphrase of the European migration crisis. Migration and the fight against causes of flight have been already areas of development policy issue since the 1960s (Stockmann et al. 2016). The highly volatile situation in 2015 politicised these issue areas on a German as well as on a European level of state development cooperation into the question of humanitarian aid and even humanitarian obligation. The immigration of asylum seekers mainly from the civil war country Syria but also from other countries of the Middle East and the African continent was at the centre of media and political attention in almost all member states of the European Union in 2015 and led to an increase of right-wing populism in most European countries (Ferenschild 2016; Thränhardt 2023). This was all the more so if these member states of the European Union had an external border of the EU as such in their national responsibility and, according to the then Dublin procedure, were actually responsible for the registration and subsequent processing of an asylum application, provided that the asylum seeker had entered the territory of the European Union there. In Germany, the sharp increase in the number of asylum seekers led to an administrative and infrastructure crisis, which was generally referred to in the media and the socio-political context as a "refugee crisis" and still is. The role of development cooperation in Germany was changed against the diverse backgrounds of this development, the associated challenges and the search for possible solutions (Ferenschild 2016).

The buzzwords "refugee crisis" and "fighting the causes of flight", as well as the increased demarcation and simultaneous blurring of conceptual and legal definitions of reasons for flight and displacement to the various forms of migration and the question of integration, have strongly influenced the BMZ ever since. In addition to the general question of the cross-cutting nature of development policy issues, stronger cooperation and confrontations with the key ministries BMI and AA are also to be expected at the level of programme implementation on the complex issue of "flight, displacement, migration, asylum". This aspect has gained even more relevance in connection with the increased numbers of people seeking protection and refugees from Afghanistan as of 2021 and especially Ukraine as of 2022 and has continued to rise (Thränhardt 2023). Moreover, this policy field does not only concern the German or European situation but also approaches of German state development cooperation in partner countries (Zintl and Loewe 2022).

The **third indicator** can be found in the policy field-immanent humanitarian discourse and the much-vaunted value-based nature of the policy field. This is the commonly associated responsibility ethic in the context of the already mentioned "refugee crisis" from 2015 and the conception of the Marshall Plan with Africa and the "Africa Year 2017". Here, crude images of development often resonate, which are based on a Western-ethnocentric image of development and are rightly often the subject of criticism (Kurer 2017; Gieler 2023). This indicator can be very vividly illustrated by symbolic representations and the very reduced and still stereotypical visual language of various state actors in development cooperation (Thiel 2001; Grill 2019; Gul 2020; Steiner 2020). This visual language can also be found in the self-presentation of the BMZ and is inherent in the present presentation of the agenda of the BMZ (BMZ 2023).

Also in published speeches and opinion pieces by the former Minister Müller but also in the placement of development policy issues in analogue and digital media as well as the chosen image and wording, this humanitarian discourse with more or less subtle value orientation or value attribution can often be found (Müller 2020). This discourse is not only related to state development cooperation but also the academic engagement with the topic, and the actions of non-state development cooperation are not free from this value discussion and stereotypes as well as the replicability of the same.[1] Whether and to what extent the BMZ actively participates in the discussion about planners or seekers related to development ideals (Easterly 2006) is an open question—but there is generally a sensitivity for the value-based nature and the intercultural challenges of this policy field (Thiel 2001; Bohnet 2015; Grill 2019; Gieler 2023).

As for the influence of the history of the BMZ on the value orientation and value-based nature of German state development cooperation in terms of a commitment to value-based development cooperation, this can be traced back to the "Spranger criteria" of 1991 (Bohnet 2017). These were and still are to be understood as a frame of reference for German state development cooperation and were further developed in 1996 and 2006 as concrete areas of action for cross-sectoral policy of the BMZ. Specifically, these criteria are the respect for human rights, the participation of the population in the political process, the guarantee of legal certainty, the existence or striving for an ecologically oriented market economy and the development orientation of the state action of the partner country.

In the context of the Millennium Development Goals, the criteria were revised in 2006 and are still reflected today in various BMZ concepts and strategies, an example being the cross-sectoral BMZ strategy for human rights policy (Bohnet 2017; Guffler et al. 2020). In the context of the Ukraine war, value-led arguments in the work of the BMZ as well as the entire German state development cooperation are taken up and also perceived as positive by the German population (Schneider et al. 2022; Zille et al. 2023). The aspect of feminist development policy in the larger framework of feminist foreign policy is very lively in theoretical discussion and the formulation of action plans and guidelines, but to what extent this point crystallises as characteristic for the value orientation of the BMZ under Minister Schulze is still open (Zilla 2022, 2023; Fröhlich and Hauschild 2023).

The **fourth indicator** is the content design and resulting performance of the ministry as well as the former Minister Müller and the present Minister Schulze. They deliberately place a strong focus on combating hunger and poverty in the world, as well as on sustainability issues and Germany's humanitarian responsibility in the question of flight and migration. The Marshall Plan with Africa and the Africa Year 2017 are inextricably linked with Gerd Müller. Thus, the fact of placing the African continent at the focus of bilateral German development cooperation with the "Reform Concept 2030" is certainly to be seen as a merit of development policy design (BMZ 2018).

Thus, a justifiable regional prioritisation takes place at the geostrategic level, which is also flanked by other approaches of German ministries and the EU. Whether the motivation is primarily humanitarian in nature or whether foreign economic or even geopolitical reasons are decisive can hardly be determined from the external perspective of the academic observer. However, for the possible perspectives of the

---

[1] The authors of this book are also aware of this issue and acknowledge it.

future design of German state development cooperation, the motivations are rather secondary—the mere fact of regional prioritisation of a continent with an inherent logical internal differentiation according to bilateral partners, reform partners, transformation partners, nexus partners and other countries according to the DAC list, which can be promoted by other instruments such as European and multilateral cooperation, promotion by civil society and cooperation with the economy, will have a lasting influence on strategic-level funding commitments, programme design and project implementation by state actors (BMZ 2018, 2020a, b).

Another aspect of this indicator is the manifold special initiatives that Müller initiated during his term of office. In addition to SEWOH as an important, perhaps overdue, focal point of German traditions in the practical implementation of development cooperation projects in the agricultural sector and the special initiatives in the aftermath of the refugee crisis, the discussion about the "Green Button" should be mentioned, as well as other "perennial issues" in the discussion about more sustainability in the production and consumption of agricultural goods and the subsequent processing of natural resources such as coffee, cocoa and bananas—but also cotton and ores (Morazan and Wulf 2018).

Here, regardless of the global discussion about WTO rules, free trade or tariff barriers, conflicts and disagreements with other federal ministries—be it the Ministry of Economy (BMWi) or the Ministry of Agriculture and Development (BMEL) and with economic and consumer associations—keep emerging. The fundamental discussion about sustainable production and consumption has only just begun in its sharpness and has been fuelled by the SDGs—and here especially SDG 12: Ensuring sustainable consumption and production patterns. The question of a company's self-commitment, i.e. voluntary participation in the form of standardised or partially standardised self-commitments based on a recognised standard and subsequent certificate versus the creation of regulatory provisions in the form of a fair and sustainable "supply chain law", was initiated during Müller's term of office and certainly represents a legacy for his successor.

In terms of the design of the implementation level, the deepening of the integration of the GIZ (Rauch 2015), which was certainly still a determining factor in his first term in the Merkel III cabinet, but can now be considered completed, is certainly worth mentioning. Compared to his predecessors, Müller has transferred the PTB and the BGR, two "new old" instruments in state development cooperation, more strongly into the development policy direction. As the PTB has been carrying out various technical cooperation projects on behalf of the BMZ since the 1960s it is older than the GTZ, which was only founded on 12 December 1974 with the start of activities of 1 January 1975. However, the PTB's areas of work in measurement, standards, testing and quality management with the aim of establishing and expanding internationally recognised quality infrastructures in emerging and developing countries and strengthening the competitiveness of partner countries in world trade were not considered a performance of development cooperation for a long time.

Therefore, the PTB, like the BGR, was missing in many overviews and summaries of the actors of state development cooperation (Andersen 2005), or the two organisations were only briefly presented—similar to, for example, CIM or the

DAAD—with reference to their special development policy area (Ihne and Wilhelm 2013; Stockmann et al. 2016). The exception in the development policy literature can be found in the study by Axel Borrmann and Reinhard Stockmann on behalf of the Federal Ministry for Economic Cooperation and Development in 2009. There, with considerable methodological effort, the evaluation systems of the individual national implementing organisations were examined, and the question of the effects of the projects and programmes they promoted was pursued (Borrmann and Stockmann 2009a, b).

This weak scientific classification applies even more strongly to the BGR as a technical-scientific federal authority in the business area of the Federal Ministry for Economy and Technology. In its own self-understanding and the presentation of the BMZ with regard to important implementing organisations, the BGR identifies itself as having been active in development cooperation in the geosector since 1958—and thus 3 years before the establishment of the BMZ and at a time when development aid was still being discussed. As of 2020, it carries out around 50 bilateral, regional and sectoral technical cooperation projects with developing and emerging countries on behalf of the BMZ on topics of mining, environmental geology, geo-resource management and dealing with geo-risks.

This stronger focus on "new old" implementing organisations is also reflected in the sixth indicator, so the focus here is more on the ministerial connection and integration of other downstream federal institutions. In this context, the role of DEval as remarkable and important should also be mentioned. Even though DEval is not an independent actor sui generis in German state development cooperation, it has the task of independently and scientifically evaluating measures of German development cooperation. The establishment of DEval as a non-profit limited liability company with the Federal Republic of Germany as the sole shareholder, represented by the BMZ, can be seen as a deepening of Niebel's initiation of the professionalisation of state development cooperation and the addressing of long-standing criticism within the framework of the OECD-DAC Peer Reviews is understood (Lücking et al 2015). With—as of 2024 – over 100 positions, 61 mostly completed evaluations, an ambitious evaluation programme 2020–2022 and a visionary institute strategy 2022–2026, DEval is certainly one of the most interesting actors for the methodological design of state development cooperation, provided the evaluations are actually used for change and adaptation learning and partnership dialogue and do not serve the ex post legitimisation of state action.

In addition to the new old organisational diversity of the implementing organisations of development cooperation—the downstream area of the BMZ—the question of the spatial location of these organisations also arises. At the latest since the move of development policy-relevant organisations such as the DIE, the DED and the DSE 1991 from Berlin to Bonn to strengthen the development policy profile of Bonn and the establishment of this objective in the course of the Bonn-Berlin Law 1994, there are several spatial clusters of German state development cooperation in the country. In addition to Bonn—which also plays a significant role in the development policy landscape as a UN location since 1995—with the headquarters of Engagement Global, DEval, DIE and GIZ, these are Berlin as the seat of the federal government and political decision centre of Germany and Frankfurt as the seat of the KfW banking group and the second headquarters of the GIZ (in addition to Bonn) in Eschborn on the city border to Frankfurt. Of subordinate interest is Cologne as the seat of the DEG, which in public perception is attributed to the greater Bonn area with the UN and other national development cooperation institutions.

The BGR as the central geoscientific advisory institution of the federal government based in Hanover and the PTB as the national metrology institute of the Federal Republic of Germany with scientific-technical service tasks and based in Braunschweig are subordinate to the Federal Ministry for Economic Affairs and Energy as the supervisory authority and are therefore rather atypical implementing organisations in projects for the BMZ. Spatially, the classic state implementing organisations in Germany concentrate on the conurbations of Cologne-Bonn, Frankfurt and Berlin, with the surrounding university cities of Darmstadt, Marburg and Giessen also being involved in the recruitment of personnel for state development cooperation and its projects—as well as the university interconnections in the Berlin area and in the Rhineland (Grundmann 2013).

Overall, the present number of state actors is similar to the much-maligned 1980s and 1990s (Stockmann et al. 2016). In the "old" West German time of the 1980s, there were the big five with GTZ, KfW, DED, CDG and DSE as well as the sixth actor, the DEG, founded in 1962 as Deutsche Gesellschaft für wirtschaftliche Zusammenarbeit mbH (which became a 100% subsidiary of the KfW banking group in 2001), and the DIE, founded in 1964. Today, there are only GIZ and KfW as state actors in the sense of the classic implementers, but also Engagement Global, PTB, BGR, DEval and DIE are relevant as state actors in the design of German development cooperation. In addition, in financial cooperation, the DEG—although a 100% subsidiary of KfW—acts as an independent actor in certain policy areas and is a strong actor in the context of the Europeanisation of development cooperation. The quality and complexity of the actors has changed significantly—however, there is little evidence of a homogeneity of development policy implementers. Although GIZ is dominant in its appearance at home and in partner countries, there are still different functional logics and target specifications between the actors.

Following on from this, the **fifth indicator** is a deepening of the already mentioned prioritisation and regionalisation of state development cooperation, specifically the stronger focus on a regional allocation and localisation of state development cooperation. The new country concept 2020 of the ministry and the associated Reform Concept 2030 was the coup de grace of a year certainly not lacking in coups and caesuras in development policy in 2020 from the perspective of German state development cooperation (Bonschab & Kappel 2020). Under the slogan "Our partner countries – a new quality of cooperation" (BMZ 2020b), the Federal Ministry for Economic Cooperation and Development has created "BMZ 2030", a comprehensive reform concept from its perspective, with the aim of using measures and resources of development policy even more strategically, effectively and efficiently.

The core of the concept, in addition to the rather functional new country list for the bilateral state development cooperation of the BMZ, is the value-based fixation of cornerstones for future cooperation with the remaining partner countries. These two core statements of the present development policy conception of the ministry are, on the one hand, an "old hat" in the development policy discussion at least since the discussion about the anchor country concept and the resulting bundling of regional cuts (Stamm 2004; Krapp and Maats 2005) and, on the other hand, also quasi-revolutionary, as long cherished traditions of international development cooperation with certain partner countries especially in Latin America now seem to be broken.

In the view of the BMZ, the new reform concept *defines a new quality of cooperation. We demand from our partner countries even stronger progress in good governance, the observance of human rights and in the fight against corruption. Initiative is the key to development. Countries that are particularly reform-oriented, we support more strongly with our reform partnerships* (BMZ 2020b).

The BMZ focuses on a concentration of development policy themes and wants to set new priorities in partnership with the spirit of the "Paris Declaration" 2005 and the often criticised High-Level Forum of Busan 2011 in climate protection, health and family policy, the establishment of sustainable supply chains, the use of digitalisation and technology transfer and the strengthening of private investments. However, this is actually nothing new in the development policy discussion—much of these approaches also resonated with the predecessors of the present Minister Schulze, mostly in speeches at international organisations or at government talks (Terre des hommes and Welthungerhilfe 2010; Bohnet 2015).

So what is genuinely "new" about the new reform concept? On the one hand, it is something that can certainly be clearly associated with the person of Minister Müller—the value-based and tangible dictum of development cooperation as poverty and hunger reduction:

> The most important goal [of the reform, note by the author] remains the overcoming of hunger and poverty in the world. (BMZ 2020b)

The second—and perhaps functionally instrumentally more revolutionary—point within the reform concept is the quasi-catch-up development related to the guiding principles of Paris, Accra and Busan—a redesign of partnership criteria and forms of international cooperation beyond political or traditional needs and sensitivities. Thus, new partnership categories are formed to protect global goods such as climate, biodiversity and human security in conflict and refugee areas, in order to effectively support partner countries (BMZ 2020b). This can also be read as a veiled admission that the traditional instruments of German state development cooperation in the past were not always precise, purposeful and effective. Also, the form and nature of cooperation of German state actors with the partner countries is changed. How exactly this happens is unclear, the reform concept is still rather nebulous and mixes here the value-based argument for a reform with the functional-instrumental argument and quite clearly states that development cooperation also after the "carrot and stick" model can be (re)designed:

> Some countries have fortunately developed in such a way that they no longer need our direct support. Others show no progress in implementing reforms. Therefore, we are

adjusting the number of partner countries with which we directly cooperate at a governmental level and reducing it from 85 to now 60. (BMZ 2020b)

In a cynical interpretation, it can also be concluded that both over- and underperformers of German governmental development cooperation will be excluded from this in the future and who ultimately is an over- or underperformer is determined by the BMZ (Bonschab & Kappel 2020). The simplicity of the reform concept at this point is therefore almost refreshing, as it shows that the sometimes enormous criticism of it is justified.

However, the BMZ also points out that within the framework of the architecture of development cooperation (Klingebiel 2013; Klingebiel 2017), the cooperation with the former partner country of governmental development cooperation is not completely ended but merely changed:

> It is important: We do not end cooperation with any country, but change the form of this cooperation. In countries with which we no longer directly cooperate at a governmental level, we strengthen the work of churches and civil society as well as the EU and multilateral institutions and promote private sector investments. (BMZ 2020b)

Further criticism of regional prioritisation is mainly based on the argument that it is not about uniform standards of human development in the socio-economic or even democratic-liberal sense but merely about achieving geostrategic goals. The traditional focus on the role of the "Least Last Developed Countries" (LLDC) with their special needs played a significantly lesser role under Development Minister Müller, unlike with many of his predecessors. Of the nine LLDCs that were removed from the list of bilateral partner countries, only two are African states, and the rest are countries in Asia and Latin America. Only South Sudan was added as a "new LLDC" to the list of bilateral partner countries and was then located in the category of nexus and peace partners in 2023.

Therefore, there is a suspicion in the developmental community, that the decisive factor—referring to individual example countries, especially on the African continent—for remaining on the list of German partner countries is less based on qualitative criteria of good governance or questions of need, but of geopolitical interests. This can be exemplified in the handling of African countries, which lie on the escape and migration routes to Europe. They continue to be valued partner countries— regardless of their often authoritarian governance and obvious violations of human rights and the principles of good governance.

Thus, there is a suspicion that double standards are being applied and the politicisation of development cooperation is advancing. After a long—sometimes bitterly led—discussion in the German development policy community and the change of government in 2021 and the clearly communicated fact that Gerd Müller will not continue to head the BMZ regardless of the outcome of the 2021 federal election, the new country concept of the BMZ was presented and fixed in 2023. Germany's total of 65 bilateral partner countries can be divided into 39 classic bilateral partners, eight transformation partnerships with countries in the EU neighbourhood (which simultaneously fall into the legal category of bilateral partners), eight global partners to achieve strategic goals of global scale and ten nexus and peace partners.

The tripartite division into bilateral partners, strategic partners and peace partners is certainly overdue from a strategic point of view, but it does create potential problems in resource allocation and is highly political from the perspective of the SDGs as well as security policy interests (Terre des hommes and Welthungerhilfe 2023; Bunde et al. 2024).

The **sixth indicator** is associated with the present and future functional-instrumental design of state development cooperation. This primarily concerns the implementing organisations in the aftermath of the BMZ and their new old role in the development policy landscape. In addition to GIZ as the leading implementing organisation of technical cooperation, only KfW Development Bank with its subsidiary, Deutsche Investitions- und Entwicklungsgesellschaft mbH, remains in financial cooperation at the strategic and operational level of implementing development cooperation programmes and projects.

Although the present BMZ leadership only slightly emphasises the existence and role of PTB and BGR as "new" actors differently than under Minister Müller, both have been actors in the state design of development cooperation for decades. The focus on domestic development policy work, development policy education and the transfer of the SDGs into the realities of life of German citizens is done through and with Engagement Global, something that has certainly contributed very positively to the change in the status of development policy in Germany since 2012.

The increased strategic use of the German Institute for Development Policy, which has existed since 1964, as a global think-tank, and of the German Evaluation Institute for Development Cooperation, founded in 2012, as a centre of methodological competence by the BMZ, is important building block for the substantive and personnel qualitative underpinning of German state development cooperation. There is also increased use of university knowledge and a sphere of development policy departmental research institutes, which partly formally in advertised projects of contract research, partly informally through their own research and scientific exchange, fuel and advance the discourse in state development cooperation. After the clear-cutting of the 1990s and noughties, with the abandonment of many development-related chairs at German universities in the course of structural reforms and savings, these are hopeful news for the future.

A systematic listing of all development policy institutes, research projects and tenders has not yet been recorded to this day. Interesting in the question of future perspectives of state development cooperation is certainly the question of whether the former scientific advisory board of the BMZ will be revived or whether the trend towards specialist commissions and advisory working groups will continue. Presently, in addition to the "One Health" advisory board in the BMZ, the expert advisory board on the "Green Button", the advisory board of the German Evaluation Institute for Development Cooperation gGmbH and the Federal Government's Commission on the Causes of Flight are active. However, the big strategic decision is no longer purely national—GIZ is heavily involved in European development cooperation and nationally and internationally both a contractor of development cooperation services and a client in the sense of subcontracting and the forwarding of funds and projects. Through its subsidiary GIZ International Services, the central

German implementing organisation in the BMZ's business area is active not only for the European Union, international organisations or the federal government but also for clients from the corporate and foundation sector and the governments of other countries.

The often mentioned new rules of the game and new actors in development cooperation are therefore already a reality at the implementation level. The question for the future is whether there is a balance of power or imbalance of power in the relationship between the BMZ and its most important implementing organisation, GIZ (Scheller and Seidler 2018). The question of control losses on the part of the BMZ and the image of GIZ as a supertanker with an unmanageable portfolio of tasks, projects and programmes is therefore certainly one of the great unknowns in the present design of state development cooperation—regardless of the recurring questions about a merger of FZ and TZ or the sharp separation of control and implementation. Much of the discussion is certainly based on the political conception and implementation of the merger in the Niebel era:

> Another core problem of development policy is its institutional fragmentation. As far as the German sector is concerned: Over time, there were KfW and DED, GTZ and DSE, CDG, InWEnt and much more. All, in doubt, with their own planning staff, sector and regional experts. So there was a lot of good, but often uncoordinated work. When the Germans moved into the partner country, the space next to the entrance portals became scarce to accommodate all the signs. And then it still had to be decided who could hang and screw on how big and how high up. So, potential for efficiency. I can keep it pleasantly short here. Today, 4 screws and one sign are enough. We have combined over 90% of the affected experts in the GIZ before 100 days of the legislative period were over. We have achieved an efficiency return of 700 positions and, by the way, also cut the salaries of the board members. We can now use part of the return to increase the political control and strategic capability of the BMZ. (Niebel 2011)

This efficiency debate within the organisation of the BMZ is very exciting to observe when looked at the adjusted key figures of the implementing organisations. The BMZ has been using the AURA organisational framework with its implementing organisations since 2002, which clarifies and distinguishes the different relationships of goals, means and resources:

> On the one hand, achieving development policy effects is the overarching goal of German development cooperation and on the other hand, the desired effects operationalised in the target system in the AURA format are also at the centre of the division of tasks between the BMZ as political control and the GIZ as implementing organisation. (Scheller and Seidler 2018, 25)

The **seventh indicator** refers to the budgetary scope of the ministry and thus of the entire state development cooperation in the context of the BMZ. Here, particular reference is made to the increasing budget of the BMZ (up to €10.2 billion in 2020 and over €12 billion in 2023). The achievement of the set goals, as far as the ODA quota is concerned, is also to be regarded as a sustained success of the policy field, as is the continuous increase in staff at the BMZ. Interestingly, the numbers of employees and specialists have also increased in most implementing organisations—the BMZ has long said goodbye to Niebel's savings dividend.

The appendix of the book goes into more detail on the corresponding numbers and statistics on this point. From a budgetary point of view, the BMZ is already an immensely important and large ministry—something that has not always correlated with its external perception in the past.

The **eighth indicator** refers to the organisational culture of the BMZ and the question of an organisational self-understanding of the ministry as an activator and interface manager of endogenous potential for global future issues (Kloke-Lesch 2016; Bohnet 2017). The discussion about a possible sustainability ministry (Bohnet 2015) in particular takes up this topic and raises important strategic questions about the future orientation of the ministry as well as the design of the entire national state development policy in the sense of policy coherence:

> Therefore, it is all the more urgent that for the four policy areas with international references, which provide a high proportion of ODA services (BMUB around eight percent of its own budget, BMZ 100 percent of its own budget, AA 33 percent of its own budget and BMBF one percent of its own budget) the coordination between the policy fields and the ODA coherence is advanced. Only then can the claim of German policy to pursue an "international policy from a single source" that addresses environmental and development issues and crisis management can be convincingly implemented. Such coherence not only increases the transparency of domestic policy and with partner countries, but also its global visibility. (Bohnet et al. 2018, 33)

An important aspect here is the factor of communication—and especially with Germany's partner countries. In relation to the "Reform 2030" and the redesign of the German partner country structure, a low point in communication has been reached (Bonschab & Kappel 2020). Partners are usually presented with a fait accompli. There were bilateral partner countries that were only informed after the decision by the BMZ. This was then not communicated in writing from the highest level but sometimes at the level of department or division heads via video link.

This aspect of communication is a diplomatic disaster and allows conclusions to be drawn about the self-image of the ministry. Obviously, the focus of communication with the partner countries is not partner-oriented but offer-oriented. The term "development aid" can still be found in both media reporting and textbooks (Kurer 2017)—even though one-sided dependency relationships in partner structures are thought to have been overcome.

In relation to the trend towards Europeanisation of development cooperation, different scenarios can be drawn up for the BMZ (Klingebiel 2017; Bohnet et al. 2018), but in terms of the BMZ's own understanding of its impact, a reassessment of the AURA concept is an obvious procedural step.

This procedural reform makes even more sense when this point is viewed from the perspective of the implementing organisations—in relation to traditional development financing, co-financing by different donors and the financing of projects to achieve the SDGs (Klingebiel 2017; Scheller et al. 2017; Martens and Ellmers 2020):

> It became clear that the BMZ's impact matrix and the EU's Description of the Action focus on different levels of objectives, as the AV illustrates – "Description of the Action is a different league than what was a bit more generic in the BMZ offer". Different philosophies

underlie this: "AURA/BMZ aims at impacts and the EU focuses more on deliverables. (Scheller et al. 2017, 40)

The **ninth and last indicator** is closely linked to the turning of the times. To what extent development cooperation is defined as a subset of civilian security policy or value-led foreign policy is a hotly debated issue against the backdrop of the war in Ukraine since 2022 (Grävingholt et al. 2023). There are many voices in the academic and practical discussion that point to the complexity of state development policy in the shaping sense and state development cooperation in the executing sense and point out the short-sightedness of this approach (Leininger and Hornidge 2024).

The important aspect of the peace focus of many development policy approaches also speaks against a new discussion about a stronger securitisation of development cooperation (Ayoob 2020), as was the case during the times of the Afghanistan engagement, a determining basic tenor of many German development policy actors (Lipovac and Nowak 2023). But the discussion about the German engagement in Afghanistan and the role of the BMZ and its implementing organisations is important for the future positioning of the BMZ in the context of networked or integrated security and Germany's national interests (Gromes 2023).

This concerns as important basic documents of the joint strategic evaluation of Germany's civilian engagement in Afghanistan (Hartmann et al. 2023) and the interim report of the Enquete Commission "Lessons from Afghanistan for Germany's future networked engagement" from 2024 (Enquete Commission 2024). Whether the BMZ can and wants to further focus as a Ministry of Peace due to results and political naivety, or whether the development policy work in crisis countries and conflict hotspots will be shifted more towards the humanitarian direction and thus into the Foreign Office, is completely open. However, it should be noted that in all crises and conflict hotspots in the world, state development cooperation is either actively involved or was until a few years ago. Given the existing country expertise in the BMZ and its implementing organisations, it would be downright negligent to do without it. This is all the more true as new global shaping powers increasingly penetrate into other policy fields from the development policy discourse and the reality of life of German citizens and everyday German politics is affected by globalisation and its downsides (Klingebiel 2017; Bunde et al. 2024).

Based on these nine indicators, the question arises about the immediate future of state development cooperation. The BMZ and its role (s) after each next federal election were always seemingly at the centre of every debate about German development cooperation. Beyond possible scenarios, the "perennial issue" of the 1990s and noughties—the question of the ministry's independence—will not necessarily be relevant. Unlike in the Heidelberg speech 2011 by former Minister Dirk Niebel, it is no longer about proving the relevance of the policy field or even getting on well with the respective Chancellor:

> I have always said: Bad development aid is no reason to abolish development policy, but to make it better. When I said years ago that the BMZ should be integrated into the AA, it was because this seemed the only way to improve. In those years, the impression was that two

ministries were pulling over each other and against each other through the world. This is no longer the case. Independent yet coordinated development policy with the AA is possible. (Niebel 2011)

Even against the backdrop of coping with the COVID-19 pandemic, there have been budget cuts in all individual plans of the ministries at the federal level. In addition, in recent years since Russia's attack on Ukraine, other investments in the BMZ budget have been reallocated or adjusted. But against the backdrop of the EU Commission's "Green Deal", the goal of an orderly European migration regime, the necessary progress in achieving the global sustainability goals and the strategic importance of numerous developing and emerging countries on the geopolitical stage, it is more likely that the policy field will gain in importance, rather than a situation where development policy would be superfluous and useless.

In summary, the nine trend indicators mentioned will certainly determine the coming decade of state development cooperation both in theory and in practical implementation. It should be noted that the indicators are not quantified and may also contradict each other in content—but human and organisational action can only be predicted on the basis of probabilities and trends:

1. Importance of international conferences and a multilateral regulatory framework for state development cooperation.
2. Development cooperation as a means of minimising flight and migration.
3. Value-bound development.
4. Professionalised organisation of the policy field by the BMZ.
5. Regionalisation of state development cooperation with a focus on countries.
6. Supply orientation of state development cooperation.
7. Financial design of state development cooperation.
8. Self-understanding of state development cooperation.
9. Development cooperation as civil security policy.

In addition to these nine indicators, other thematic-content interfaces with other ministries appear to be of particular relevance for the design of state development cooperation, in which the BMZ should or even must clearly position itself in the future (Bohnet 2017):

> In addition to the BMZ, over the years other ministries have developed an "ODA arm". The increase in international tasks is also reflected at the level of the individual ministries. They have created their own departments and divisions that operate public development cooperation with their own budgets. The ODA services of the federal ministries (except BMZ) have continuously increased over the past 20 years. They amounted to 2 billion euros in 2015 and thus made up 13 percent of total ODA. The main ODA donors are the AA, the BMUB, the BMBF and recently also the BMF and the BKM. (Bohnet et al. 2018; 12)

In this context, the methodological—and conceptual—question of the relevance of the ODA quota in the future as a relevant and meaningful measure for development policy interventions and the implications thereof for project design in development cooperation (Severino and Ray 2009; Klingebiel 2017) are open and field of discuission. This goes hand in hand with questions of multilateral cooperation, new partnership control instruments and thus a likely paradigm shift in the process of implementation and achievement of the SDGs (Fouré et al. 2013; Atwood 2017; Klingebiel 2017, 2020; Martens and Ellmers 2020). It should be noted that the ninth trend indicator can massively change these interface topics. A BMZ, which manages more strategically as an element of German soft power resources, initiates programmes, implements projects and promotes or prevents access to non-state actors, is—next to the Foreign Office and the Federal Ministry of Defence—a not to be underestimated actor of national security interests and their global enforcement.

At the national German level, these interface topics with the other internationally active ministries at the federal level are likely to be the following in the coming time:

1. The (out)design of the topic *Migration* (in distinction to AA and BMI).
2. The *cooperation with African states* and a holistic Africa approach (in distinction to AA, BMWi, BMBF, BKM and BMF).
3. The *implementation of the SDGs* nationally and internationally (in distinction to the Chancellery as "custodian agency" as well as BMUB).

These trends are changing the German ODA profile. Similar developments can be observed with other DAC donors, as in addition to the ministries responsible for development policy, other ministries are increasingly involved in development cooperation. The share of humanitarian aid and the ODA-eligible refugee expenditures has also increased significantly among other donors. For the strategic debate in Germany, these changes result in an important conclusion: The changes should be consciously perceived by politics and the public. Technical debates especially in the German Bundestag and in its specialist committees can contribute to understanding, classifying and possibly shaping the changes – for example in the allocation of public funds. for ODA tasks to different actors. In particular, it should be about capturing the opportunities, challenges and potential risks of structural changes more precisely, so that the federal government and parliament can further improve Germany's development cooperation with their decisions. (Bohnet et al. 2018, 35)

References

Andersen, U. (2005): *Informationen zur politischen Bildung. Entwicklung und Entwicklungspolitik*, Nr. 259/2005. Bonn.

Atwood, J. B. (2017). *Applied history: Still Learning from 60 years of Development Co-operation*. Vortrag im Rahmen der 23. Käte Hamburger Lecture, 17. Mai 2017 in Duisburg.

Ayoob, M. (2020). The UN and North-South Relations in the Security Arena. In: *Global Governance 26/2*, 251-261.

BMZ – Bundesministerium für wirtschaftliche Zusammenarbeit und Entwicklung. (2015). *Zukunftscharta EINE Welt – Unsere Verantwortung*. Bonn und Berlin.

BMZ – Bundesministerium für wirtschaftliche Zusammenarbeit und Entwicklung. (2017). *Der Zukunftsvertrag für die Welt Die Agenda 2030 für nachhaltige Entwicklung*. Bonn und Berlin.

BMZ – Bundesministerium für wirtschaftliche Zusammenarbeit und Entwicklung (2018). *Entwicklungspolitik 2030: Neue Herausforderungen – neue Antworten*. Bonn.

BMZ – Bundesministerium für wirtschaftliche Zusammenarbeit und Entwicklung. (2020a). *Gemeinsam weiter – Zukunft denken*. Bonn und Berlin.

BMZ – Bundesministerium für wirtschaftliche Zusammenarbeit und Entwicklung. (2020b). *Reformkonzept „BMZ 2030" Umdenken – Umsteuern*. Bonn und Berlin.

BMZ – Bundesministerium für wirtschaftliche Zusammenarbeit und Entwicklung (2023). *BMZ-Agenda für gute Arbeit weltweit*. Bonn & Berlin.

Bohnet, M. (2015). *Geschichte der deutschen Entwicklungspolitik. Strategien, Innenansichten, Zeitzeugen, Herausforderungen*; Konstanz.

Bohnet, M. (2017). *Politische Ökonomie der deutschen Entwicklungszusammenarbeit. Bestimmungsmuster, Akteure und Allokationsmuster*. DIE Discussion Paper 20/2017. Bonn.

Bohnet, M., Klingebiel, S., & Marschall, P. (2018). Die Struktur der deutschen öffentlichen Entwicklungszusammenarbeit – Hintergründe, Trends und Implikationen für das BMZ und andere Bundesressorts. *DIE Discussion Paper 15/2018*. Bonn.

Bonschab, T., & Kappel, R. (2020). Entwicklungspolitik Made in BMZ 2030. Blogbeitrag, unter: https://weltneuvermessung.wordpress.com/2020/07/13/entwicklungspolitik-made-in-bmz-2030/. Zugegriffen: 04.01.2021.

Borrmann, A., & Stockmann, R. (2009a). *Evaluation in der deutschen Entwicklungszusammenarbeit: Band 1: Systemanalyse*. Münster.

Borrmann, A., & Stockmann, R. (2009b). *Evaluation in der deutschen Entwicklungszusammenarbeit: Band 2: Fallstudien*. Münster.

Bunde, T./ Eisentraut, S./ Schütte, L. (Hrsg.) (2024). *Munich Security Report 2024: Lose-Lose?* München.

Easterly, W. (2006): *Wir retten die Welt zu Tode. Für ein professionelleres Management im Kampf gegen die Armut*, Frankfurt/New York.

Enquete-Kommission Lehren aus Afghanistan für das künftige vernetzte Engagement Deutschlands (Hrsg.) (2024). *Zwischenbericht der Enquete-Kommission Lehren aus Afghanistan für das künftige vernetzte Engagement Deutschlands*. Drucksache 20/10400 des Deutschen Bundestags, 20. Wahlperiode. Berlin.

Ferenschild, S. (2016): *Migration global*. Bonn.

Fouré, J., Bénassy-Quéré, A., & Fontagné, L. (2013). Modelling the world economy at the 2050 horizon. In: *Economics of Transition, 21(4)*, 617-654.

Fröhlich, M. & Hauschild, A. (2023). Feministische Außenpolitik. In: In: *Aus Politik und Zeitgeschichte (APuZ) 73 (13)*, 34–39.

Gieler, W. (2023). *Reguliertes Chaos: (Re-)Konstruktionen zum westlichen Ethnozentrismus* (2nd ed.). Bonn.

Gönner, T. (2022). Sicherheit durch Nachhaltigkeit – Vernetzt arbeiten für eine krisenfestere Welt. In: Behörden Spiegel-Gruppe in Zusammenarbeit mit dem Bundesverband der Deutschen Sicherheits- und Verteidigungsindustrie e.V. (BDSV) (Hrsg.): *Frieden, Sicherheit, Nachhaltigkeit – Beiträge zu einer gesellschaftspolitischen Debatte*. Bonn. 30–31.

Grävingholt, J., Faust, J., Libman, A., Richter, S., Sasse, G., & Stewart, S. (2023). Wiederaufbau in der Ukraine: Was die internationale Gemeinschaft jetzt beachten muss (*IDOS Policy Brief 2/2023*). Bonn.

Grill, B. (2019): *Wir Herrenmenschen. Unser rassistisches Erbe: Eine Reise in die deutsche Kolonialgeschichte*, München.

Gromes, T. (2023). Scheitern in Afghanistan: Wenn es sich Ursachenforschung zu einfach macht. *PRIF Spotlight 11/2023*. Frankfurt am Main.

Grundmann, G. (2013). *Internationale Entwicklungszusammenarbeit als Berufsfeld*, Berlin.

Guffler, K., Harutyunyan, A., DiLorenzo, M., Sethi, T., Eppler, E., Heinelt M.S. (2020). *Development Cooperation from a Partner Perspective. How can Germany and other donors perform better in the eyes of their partner countries?* Bonn.

Gul, M. (2020): „Von ‚Unterentwicklung' zu SDGs", in: *E+Z Entwicklung und Zusammenarbeit, Jg. 61, 09-10/2020*, 20.

Hartmann, C. (2012): „Entwicklungspolitik im Wandel: „Neuerfindung" oder neue Bescheidenheit?", in: Andersen, Uwe (Hrsg.): *Entwicklungspolitik. Standortbestimmung, Kritik und Perspektiven,* (13-28). Schwalbach/Ts.

Hartmann, C., Roxin, H., Atal, M.R., Berchtold, H., Kellogg, M., Weeger, M. & Zürcher, C. (2023). *Ressortgemeinsame strategische Evaluierung des zivilen Engagements der Bundesregierung in Afghanistan. Ressortspezifischer Bericht zum Engagement des BMZ in Afghanistan.* Deutsches Evaluierungsinstitut der Entwicklungszusammenarbeit (DEval). Bonn.

Ihne, H. &Wilhelm, J. (Hrsg.) (2013): *Einführung in die Entwicklungspolitik,* Bonn.

Kerkow, U. (2017). *Ländersache Nachhaltigkeit – Die Umsetzung der 2030-Agenda für nachhaltige Entwicklung durch die Bundesländer.* Bonn.

Klingebiel, S. (2013). *Entwicklungszusammenarbeit – Eine Einführung.* Bonn.

Klingebiel, S. (2017): „Entwicklungspolitik in turbulenten Zeiten. Neuorientierung im Kontext von Krisen und strukturellem Wandel", in: *Wirtschaftspolitische Blätter 3/2017,* 349-359.

Klingebiel, S. (2020). *The Palgrave Handbook of Development Cooperation for Achieving the 2030 Agenda – Contested Collaboration,* London.

Kloke-Lesch, A. (2016). Globale Entwicklungspolitik – Politikberatung zwischen Aid-Community und Global Public Policy. In S. Falk et al. (Hrsg.), *Handbuch Politikberatung* (417–434). Wiesbaden.

Krapp, S., & Maats, P. (2005). *Ansätze für Länderprogrammevaluationen – Eine Vergleichende Kurzanalyse.* Saarbrücken.

Kurer, O. (2017): *Entwicklungspolitik heute. Lassen sich Wohlstand und Wachstum planen?.* Wiesbaden.

Leininger, J. & Hornidge, A. (2024). Sicherheitspolitik ist nicht Entwicklungspolitik *(Die aktuelle Kolumne 19.02.2024).* Bonn.

Lipovac, S. & Nowak, M. (2023). Afghanistan. In: Gieler, W. & Nowak, M. (Hrsg.): *Deutsche Entwicklungszusammenarbeit im Spannungsfeld der Außen- und Sicherheitspolitik: Frieden – Sicherheit – Entwicklung.* Wiesbaden. 265-286.

Lücking, K., Freund, S., & Bettighofer, B. (2015). *Evaluierungspraxis in der deutschen Entwicklungszusammenarbeit. Umsetzungsmonitoring der letzten Systemprüfung und Charakterisierung wesentlicher Elemente.* Bonn.

Martens, J. & Ellmers, B. (2020). *Agenda 2030: Wo steht die Welt? 5 Jahre SDGs – eine Zwischenbilanz,* Bonn.

Martens, J. & Obenland, W. (2017). *Die Agenda 2030. Globale Zukunftsziele für nachhaltige Entwicklung,* Vollständig aktualisierte und überarbeitete Neuauflage 2017. Bonn.

Martens, J. & Scherer, J. (2021). *Baustellen des Multilateralismus.* Bonn.

Morazan, P., & Wulf, P. (2018). Ausgerechnet Bananen: Wer zahlt den Preis für das Sonderangebot? *SÜDWIND Factsheet.* Bonn.

Müller, G. (2020). *Umdenken. Überlebensfragen der Menschheit.* Hamburg.

Niebel, D. (2011). Entwicklungspolitik als Zukunftspolitik, Heidelberger Rede zur Zukunft der deutschen Entwicklungspolitik, Universität Heidelberg, 8. November 2011.

Rauch, T. (2015). Zur Reform der deutschen Entwicklungszusammenarbeit, in: *Aus Politik und Zeitgeschichte, 65. Jahrgang 7–9/2015.* 36–42.

Scheller, O., & Seidler, M. (2018). *Externe Qualitätskontrolle der GIZ. Ergebnisbericht 2017.* Berlin.

Scheller, O., Kruse, A.-M., & Freimann, I. (2017). *USE Kofinanzierung.* Bonn.

Schneider, S. H. et al. (2022). *Meinungsmonitor Entwicklungspolitik 2022. Entwicklungspolitisches Engagement in Zeiten globaler Krisen und Herausforderungen.* Deutsches Evaluierungsinstitut der Entwicklungszusammenarbeit (DEval). Bonn.

Severino, J.-M., & Ray, O. (2009). The End of ODA: Death and Rebirth of a Global Public Policy. *CGD Working Paper 167.* Washington, D.C.

Stamm, A. (2004). Schwellen- und Ankerländer als Akteure einer globalen Partnerschaft – Überlegungen zu einer Positionsbestimmung aus deutscher entwicklungspolitischer Sicht. *DIE Discussion Paper 01/2004.* Bonn.

Steiner, A. (2020): „UNDP. Governance hat zentrale Bedeutung", in: *E+Z Entwicklung und Zusammenarbeit, Jg. 61, 09-10/2020*, 21–23.

Stockmann, R., Menzel, U., & Nuscheler, F. (2016). *Entwicklungspolitik. Theorien – Probleme – Strategien*, 2nd ed., München.

Terre des hommes & Welthungerhilfe (2010). *Die Wirklichkeit der Entwicklungspolitik 2010. Eine kritische Bestandsaufnahme der deutschen Entwicklungszusammenarbeit. Achtzehnter Bericht: „Profitable Partnerschaft? Entwicklungszusammenarbeit mit der deutschen Wirtschaft"*. Bonn.

Terre des hommes & Welthungerhilfe (2023). *Kompass 2023: Wirklichkeit der Deutschen Entwicklungspolitik. Forderungen an die deutsche Entwicklungspolitik*. Bonn.

Thiel, R. E. (Hrsg.) (2001). *Neue Ansätze zur Entwicklungstheorie*, Bonn.

Thränhardt, D. (2023). Mit offenen Armen – die kooperative Aufnahme von Kriegsflüchtlingen aus der Ukraine in Europa Eine Alternative zum Asylregime? Bonn

Wege, S. (2023). Sicherheitspolitik in den SDGs. In: Gieler, W. & Nowak, M. (Hrsg.): *Deutsche Entwicklungszusammenarbeit im Spannungsfeld der Außen- und Sicherheitspolitik: Frieden – Sicherheit – Entwicklung*. Wiesbaden. 97–114.

Wieczorek-Zeul, H. (2017). Entwicklungspolitik im 21. Jahrhundert. Die Sustainable Development Goals. In: Burchardt, H.-J., Peters, S., Weinmann, N. (Hrsg.): *Entwicklungstheorie von heute – Entwicklungspolitik von morgen*. Baden-Baden. 49–58.

Zilla, C. (2022). Feministische Außenpolitik – Konzepte, Kernelemente und Kontroversen. *SWP-Aktuell 2022/A 50*. Berlin.

Zilla, C. (2023). *Neuausrichtung der Außenpolitik. Feministische Außen- und Entwicklungspolitik in Ressortpapieren und in der Debatte*. SWP. Berlin.

Zille, H., Gödderz, A., Schneider S.H. & Bruder, M. (2023). Entwicklungspolitische Einstellungen im Kontext des Krieges gegen die Ukraine. *DEval Policy Brief 9/2023*. Deutsches Evaluierungsinstitut der Entwicklungszusammenarbeit (DEval). Bonn.

Zintl, T. & Loewe, M (2022). More than the sum of its parts: donor-sponsored cash-for-work programmes and social cohesion in Jordanian communities hosting Syrian refugees. In: *The European Journal of Development Research, 34 (3)*. 1320–1357.

Appendix

The following tables and figures illustrate the challenges of ODA (Official Development Assistance) in the design and implementation of German state development cooperation. These data show trends that are related to the challenge of a relational goal that is in relation to Germany's gross national income and continues to shape the political discourse.

Since 2018, due to increasing methodological criticism of the ODA figure as the sole indicator for development-related payments between different countries, a new calculation method for the ODA value of preferential loans has been introduced. This new methodology was first applied to the data for 2018, which includes public loans and loans to multilateral institutions. It is referred to as the "grant equivalent method" and is based on the reporting of the grant equivalent of loans, which is calculated on the basis of donor expenditure.

Regardless of the calculation methodology from 2018, until the Corona pandemic, the increase in their expenditure for development within 5 years to 0.7% of gross national income, promised by Germany and other donor countries at the United Nations General Assembly on 24 October 1970, was only actually achieved in 1 year. This was in 2016. This was caused by effects of taking into account domestic expenditure for refugees, and thus Germany had actually achieved the 0.7% target for the first time. Due to the eligibility of expenditure for the multiple crisis bundles and services in the areas of flight and migration, climate and environment, and health, Germany has achieved its self-set target every year since 2020.

For the reporting year 2022, Germany has recorded ODA services eligible for calculation by Destatis and the OECD amounting to 33.9 billion euros (in 2021 it was still 28.1 billion euros). Of this, 26.9 billion euros was for bilateral and 7.0 billion euros for multilateral cooperation – of which almost 40% are located in the

© The Author(s), under exclusive license to Springer Fachmedien Wiesbaden GmbH, part of Springer Nature 2024
W. Gieler, M. Nowak (eds.), *Understanding German Development Cooperation*, Contributions to Political Science, https://doi.org/10.1007/978-3-658-45596-5

business area of the BMZ. In contrast, the 1990s were a low point for the ODA quota in Germany, with only 0.3% in ODA funds.

In the German context, the ratio of ODA funds (Official Development Assistance) for bilateral and multilateral activities is of particular interest. Germany describes itself as a "champion of multilateralism" and uses a large part of its funds for development cooperation bilaterally, that is, directly with individual partner countries.

A look at the development of this ratio is revealing: In 2004, the ratio of bilateral to multilateral ODA expenditures was almost balanced. Since then, however, there has been a significant decline in multilateral ODA expenditures in relation to total expenditures. This trend is both significant and noteworthy as it indicates changes in the strategic orientation and prioritisation of German development cooperation.

The increase in bilateral funding compared to multilateral funds may reflect a targeted focus on specific partnerships and projects where Germany can exert direct influence and control. This could also be due to an increased emphasis on national interests and priorities in development cooperation.

At the same time, this trend raises questions about the effectiveness and efficiency of bilateral compared to multilateral development aid approaches. Multilateral approaches often have the advantage of scalability, coordination and broader international cooperation, while bilateral approaches can enable more targeted and flexible implementation.

The analysis of this ratio provides insights into development policy and Germany's strategic orientation in the field of development cooperation as well as into the dynamics of multilateral engagement in the global context. It is an important topic for the discussion about the effectiveness and orientation of international development aid efforts.

Despite the official cessation of formal development cooperation with China under Minister Niebel, significant contributions from the Federal Ministry for Economic Cooperation and Development (BMZ) with China are still included in the ODA statistics. This circumstance can be attributed to the complex structure of the OECD financial architecture, which places specific requirements on reporting and financing modalities of international cooperation.

The inclusion of ODA-relevant services of the BMZ in the statistics despite the formal end of development cooperation with China could be due to several factors. On the one hand, it may be that certain projects or programmes of the BMZ in China are still classified as relevant to development cooperation because they pursue certain development policy objectives, such as poverty reduction or environmental protection.

Another reason could lie in the specific reporting requirements of the OECD, which can also take into account services that are not directly assigned to formal development cooperation but are nevertheless considered to be development-promoting.

Additionally, financing modalities play a role. Often, certain projects or activities are carried out within the framework of bilateral or multilateral financing agreements, which can still be considered ODA-relevant despite the formal end of development cooperation with China.

The complex nature of the OECD financial architecture, including the strict reporting requirements and the broad definition of ODA, leads to certain services of the BMZ with China continuing to appear in the official ODA statistics, even though formal development cooperation has been discontinued. This illustrates the challenges in delimiting and reporting on development cooperation in an international context with different financing and cooperation models.

The list of the top ten recipient countries provides a detailed overview of the priority countries of German state development cooperation based on absolute figures. This list shows which countries are the largest recipients of development aid from Germany and thus reflects the regional priorities that illustrate the prevailing trends in German development cooperation.

The choice of 5-year intervals for the analysis has several reasons. On the one hand, this allows to escape the logic of legislative periods, as political goals and priorities can often change within these 5-year periods. By using 5-year periods, the data is also analysed in an appropriate time frame without the intervals between the periods considered becoming too large, enabling a meaningful analysis based on decades.

This periodic analysis provides insight into the development of the focus regions of German development cooperation over time. It allows tracking changes in recipient countries and the extent of German development aid over the years and identifying trends as well as long-term strategic decisions in development policy.

By looking at the top ten recipient countries in 5-year intervals, patterns and developments can also be recognised that go beyond short-term fluctuations and enable a sound analysis of the long-term orientation of German development cooperation. This is crucial to assess the effectiveness and impact of German development aid and to inform future measures and strategies (Tables A1, A2, A3, A4, and A5).

Table A1 Overview of the ministers

Name	Term of office	Life data	Cabinet	Party
Walter Scheel	1961–1966	*08/07/1919 in Solingen †24/08/2016 in Bad Krozingen	Adenauer IV, Adenauer V, Erhard I, Erhard II	FDP
Werner Dollinger	1966	*18/10/1918 in Neustadt/Aich †03/01/2008 in Neustadt/Aich	Erhard II	CSU
Hans-Jürgen Wischnewski	1966–1968	*24/07/1922 in Allenstein †24/02/2005 in Cologne	Kiesinger	SPD
Erhard Eppler	1968–1974	*09/12/1926 in Ulm †19/10/2019 in Schwäbisch Hall	Kiesinger, Brandt I, Brandt II, Schmidt I	SPD
Egon Bahr	1974–1976	*18/03/1922 in Treffurt/Werra †19/08/2015 in Berlin	Schmidt I	SPD
Marie Schlei	1976–1978	*26/11/1919 in Reetz (Recz) †21/05/1983 in Berlin	Schmidt II	SPD
Rainer Offergeld	1978–1982	*26/12/1937 in Genoa/Italy	Schmidt II, Schmidt III	SPD
Jürgen Warnke	1982–1987	*20/03/1932 in Berlin †27/04/2013 in Klanxbüll	Kohl I, Kohl II, Kohl III	SPD
Hans Klein	1987–1989	*11/07/1931 in M.-Schönberg (Šumperk) †26/11/1996 in Bonn	Kohl III	CSU
Jürgen Warnke	1989–1991	*20/03/1932 in Berlin †27/04/2013 in Klanxbüll	Kohl III, Kohl IV	SPD
Carl-Dieter Spranger	1991–1998	*28.03.1939 in Leipzig	Kohl IV, Kohl V	CSU
Heidemarie Wieczorek-Zeul	1998–2009	*21/11/1942 in Frankfurt a.M.	Schröder I, Schröder II, Merkel I	SPD
Dirk Niebel	2009–2013	*29/03/1963 in Hamburg	Merkel II	FDP
Gerd Müller	2013–2021	*25/08/1955 in Krumbach	Merkel III, Merkel IV	CSU
Svenja Schulze	Since 2021	*29/09/1968 in Düsseldorf	Scholz	SPD

Table A2 2020—aid (ODA total net) disbursements to countries and regions

#	Country	In thousand $
1	Syria	$ 791.49
2	India	$ 574.65
3	Jordan	$ 529.39
4	Iraq	$ 525.16
5	People's Republic of China	$ 522.04
6	Afghanistan	$ 423.33
7	Mexico	$ 305.90
8	Turkey	$ 289.36
9	Tunisia	$ 273.91
10	Yemen	$ 250.17

Source https://stats.oecd.org/#

Table A3 2015—aid (ODA total net) disbursements to countries and regions

#	Country	In thousand $
1	India	$ 830.00
2	People's Republic of China	$ 601.97
3	Republic of South Africa	$ 427.50
4	Ukraine	$ 411.22
5	Afghanistan	$ 399.83
6	Morocco	$ 388.62
7	Turkey	$ 352.86
8	Indonesia	$ 343.95
9	Syria	$ 306.00
10	Brazil	$ 297.54

Source https://stats.oecd.org/#

Table A4 2010—aid (ODA total net) disbursements to countries and regions

#	Country	In thousand $
1	Afghanistan	$ 470.96
2	India	$ 397.95
3	People's Republic of China	$ 322.32
4	Brazil	$ 248.08
5	Pakistan	$ 142.46
6	Tanzania	$ 134.82
7	Serbia	$ 126.58
8	Palestine (Western Jordan and Gaza)	$ 104.85
9	Egypt	$ 104.76
10	Ethiopia	$ 96.70

Source https://stats.oecd.org/#

Table A5 2000—aid (ODA total net) disbursements to countries and regions

#	Country	In thousand $
1	People's Republic of China	$ 342.32
2	Zambia	$ 180.53
3	Serbia	$ 158.68
4	Bosnia and Herzegovina	$ 147.20
5	Egypt	$ 104.81
6	Brazil	$ 79.56
7	Mozambique	$ 76.82
8	Cameroon	$ 75.54
9	Bolivia	$ 72.93
10	Jordan	$ 71.23

Source https://stats.oecd.org/#